Past Poets
– Future Voices

2010 Poetry Competition for 11-18 year-olds

Poems From The UK

Edited by Amy Brownlie

First published in Great Britain in 2010 by

 Young**Writers**

Remus House
Coltsfoot Drive
Peterborough
PE2 9JX
Telephone: 01733 890066
Website: www.youngwriters.co.uk

Foreword

Young Writers was established in order to promote creativity and a love of reading and writing in children and young adults. We believe that by offering them a chance to see their own work in print, their confidence will grow and they will be encouraged to become the poets of tomorrow.

Our latest competition 'Past Poets - Future Voices' was specifically designed as a showcase for secondary school pupils, giving them a platform with which to express their ideas, aspirations and passions. In order to expand their skills, entrants were encouraged to use different forms, styles and techniques.

Selecting the poems for publication was a difficult yet rewarding task and we are proud to present the resulting anthology. We hope you agree that this collection is an excellent insight into the voices of the future.

Contents

Norton Hill School, Radstock

Oxclose Community School, Washington

Priory Community School, Weston-Super-Mare

Ryton Comprehensive School, Ryton

St Gregory's RC School, Bath

South Wilts Grammar School, Salisbury

The Crypt School, Gloucester

The Poems

My Big Brother

From day one all we did was fight,
Now all I do is fight back my tears.
I want to do everything you do
Because I want to be just like you.
Now I sit here wondering what to do
Because there's no one who can ever replace you.
I never told you how I really felt,
Like how much I really didn't hate you.

You encouraged me in everything I did and do,
You were my best friend and my number one hero.
I used to get annoyed at the sound of your guitar,
Or your midnight calls to girlfriends.
I miss our nonsense arguments,
I still like to remember the good times and bad.
I regret all the times I shouted at you
When you were just trying to help,
But you know I only did it because it's my job.

Sometimes I hurt and wonder why.
What did I do to deserve this stupid life?
Does God hate me or is this just a game?
The game of living, it's all the same.
When I close my eyes I can see you,
I can tell you watch everything I do.
If only I could have stopped that car,
But the thing was, you were too far.

You needed my help when I just wasn't there,
You gave us all a massive scare.
We were all worried and I want you to know,
If I had the choice I wouldn't let you go.
What I'm trying to say is,
I love you forever and each day.

Becky Evans (13)

1

Raindrops

Pitter
    Patter

A relaxing natural beat
Rain on my window
Or could it be?
The sound of tiny feet

Pitter
    Patter

It comes down in sheets
It doesn't differentiate
It doesn't turn a cheek
It dampens both the fair and the cheats

Pitter
    Patter

Everything streaked with God's wet brush
Droplets racing down the windowpane
No matter how many times we watch
It always causes a pin-drop hush

Pitter
    Patter

Why don't you come endure?
The ultimate cleansing
Outside in the rain
It should be mandatory written into the law

Pitter
    Patter.

Jack Watson (16)

2

Aglow

It's all it takes
Spilled sweet and fresh
From a feeling that
Compassion aches to pass on
A gift totally unexpected
And quite unasked for, a glow
Slipped into the fading light
By something beautiful, eyes beam with it
Sparkling and dancing like
Honeybees and champagne.
Almost a scent
Warmed from resting close
To the heart, easily spilt
Lighting the way home,
Spreading into the evening
Air like fairy dust.
A glow slipped from
Person to person
Woven with love
Helping smooth the surface
Of old wounds and hurts
A healer, untraceable, builds
Stronger bridges than steel
With a touch that's gentle
There's no sweeter thing
Than the kindness that's a glow in a
Smile.

Rebecca Childs (17)

3

My Life

In the house there is always a rush,
Why does my sister want to blush?
With all that make-up on her face
She looks a huge disgrace.
Nobody wants to get out of bed today,
That is why I have to say,
'Get up.'

Now we have to go to school,
That is why I have to look cool.
Hi, that's my friends over there,
Everyone with spiked-up hair.
That's the bell, have to dash,
Don't want to be late for class.
Bye.

PE, English, French and maths,
So this is why people hate class.
Yes, it's lunchtime,
Now it's time to take the climb.
Up and up the ladder I go,
I hope I get that part in the school show.
Wheeeeeeeeee!

Back to the house I go,
Now that is the end of my show,
Bye!

Verse Abudar (11)

A Time For Everything

To everything there is a season
A time to live and a time to die
A time to be a child, a time to grow up
A time to be bored, a time to have fun
A time to laugh, a time to cry
A time for happiness, a time for sadness
A time for hurt and a time for joy
A time for love and a time for hate
A time to be shy, a time to be enthusiastic
A time to try, a time to fail
A time to give, a time to be selfish
A time to lose, a time to win
A time to talk, a time to listen
A time to fall out and a time to be friends
A time to give advice, a time to hold back
A time to be honest, a time to lie
A time for night and a time for day
There is a time for everything.

Emma Wyatt (12)
Airdrie Academy, Airdrie

A Friend Like You!

A friend is someone who is there for you,
Who, when you're down, will make you smile.
A friend is someone you can talk to
And gossip with for a while.

A friend is someone to have a laugh with,
Who makes you laugh like a hyena.
A friend is someone to confide in,
She will be there when you need her.

My friend, you love to have fun,
You're hyper, like a kangaroo,
And for all of the reasons above,
I'm glad I've got a friend like you.

Hollie Neeson (13)
Airdrie Academy, Airdrie

5

To Everything There Is A Season

To everything there is a season,
A time to be born, a time to laugh,
A time to cry, a time for rejoicing,
A time for meeting new friends and a time for friendships ending,
A time for enjoyment and a time for disappointment,
A time for destiny and a time for what the future holds,
A time for free will and a time for obedience,
A time for adventure and a time for doubt,
A time for being the person you really are,
A time for regret and a time for the happiest of days,
Sadly a time for goodbyes and a time for parting,
And finally a time for eternal rest for all time.
If you want the time back just remember the saying of the Buddha:
For those who wish time they must make time
To ensure they have the time of their life.

Marion Anderson (13)
Airdrie Academy, Airdrie

To Everything There Is A Season

To everything there is a season,
A time for everything under the sun,
A time to be helpless and a time to be strong,
A time to walk with family and a time to walk alone,
A time to hide and a time to seek,
A time to be parted from friends and a time to make new friends,
A time to laugh and a time to cry,
A time to be proud and a time to be ashamed,
A time to lead and a time to be led,
A time to wake and a time to sleep,
A time to fight and a time to forgive,
A time to love and a time to hate,
A time to talk and a time to listen to others,
A time to be born and a time to die.

Eilidh Dickson (13)
Airdrie Academy, Airdrie

Jack

In the past of eighteen eighty-eight,
Six women were brutally murdered.
To the police 'twas an utter mystery,
No links between the victims,
Except all of them were women.
This trophy killer butchered them all
And took an organ or two.
Each murder took only fifteen minutes
And the police were left no clue.
He called himself Jack the Ripper,
And his name was very true,
And to this day
He has not been caught,
Turning in his grave
He could have one other thought.

Poppy-Victoria Adams (13)
Ansford School, Castle Cary

It's About The World We Live In

You're on the world, you look up high
You see the starry, moonlit sky,
It's about the world we live in.

Children in school, educated well
People in work find goods to sell,
It's about the world we live in.

Life is a scare
But the world isn't fair.
It's about the world we live in.

It's not about the law,
It's not about the trust,
In the end
It's about the world we live in.

Chloe Sage (13)
Ansford School, Castle Cary

7

What Is This?

What is this I see before me?
Dry, parched places,
Starving, ill faces,
This is what the world's turned out to be.

What is this I see before me?
Dying, crying babies,
A mind full of maybes,
This is the world, don't you see?

What is this I see before me?
A world lacking trust,
Where war is a must.
This is what our world's turned out to be.

Ellen Talbot (13)
Ansford School, Castle Cary

Upon My Boat

On a small boat on the sea
We are all resting
Until the storm crowds round the boat.
The wind is rushing, I had better get my coat.
With howling of wind
And rushing rain.

It's suddenly calm on my boat
The sun has come out
The rain has stopped
Upon my small boat the sun is shining.

Chloe Holloway (13)
Ansford School, Castle Cary

8

An Umbrella To The Sky

An umbrella to the sky.
I hold my head up high,
Don my wellies, coat and hat
And step to meet my front door mat.
Outside I see the rain through the frosted windowpane.
I clench the handle tightly as I pull back the door,
What awaits me, to be honest, I just can't quite be sure.
But as the door swings open
And the biting wind comes near,
I think, *maybe not today, I'd rather stay in here.*

Mabel Bachini (13)
Ansford School, Castle Cary

In My Meadow

The long, delicate grass
Swayed from side to side

While watching a floret
Slowly die

I sat under
My willow tree

Ancient and encrusted
But I love thee.

Harriet Chainey (13)
Ansford School, Castle Cary

The Green Steam Train

So much depends upon
The green steam train
Filled with many people
Beside the blue sea.

Stephen Jarrett (13)
Ansford School, Castle Cary

9

Daisy

Sitting there so proud,
Her eyes shut tight.
She is not loud
But she is quite bright.

Her name is Daisy,
She is quite lazy.
I could have called her Maisy,
But that would be crazy.

Eden Hamblin (13)
Ansford School, Castle Cary

Night

When the sun's asleep, out comes the moon,
A mysterious light shines upon the town.
All is quiet, everyone's asleep,
Apart from a sly fox who is chasing after a rabbit,
Unable to see much but still keeping close to its prey.
Until the sun comes up, all is dark and quiet,
Everyone's asleep.

Jasmine Bugler (14)
Ansford School, Castle Cary

My Beautiful Girlfriend

Jessica Benice Whetstone,
I love it when she calls me on the phone.
She is my beautiful girlfriend
And I never want us to end.
I love her like a fat lad loves cake,
I know our love is not fake.
She is my beautiful girlfriend.

Merrie Crozier (13)
Ansford School, Castle Cary

She Is Mine

She is beautiful in every single way,
Her hair, her eyes, her voice, her everything.
I love the way her hair blows in the wind.
I love the way her eyes sparkle in the night.
She is my beautiful girlfriend forever,
She is my best friend always.
She is mine.

Jessi Whetstone (14)
Ansford School, Castle Cary

Daisy

Loves me, loves me not.
Why do you pull my petals off?
I know not what you talk about
Nor who loves you or does not.

Belladonna Barrington-Jones (13)
Ansford School, Castle Cary

The Homeless Monkey

So much depends upon
The homeless, smelly monkey
Wearing a pink tie
Beside the interview room.

Thomas Cox (13)
Ansford School, Castle Cary

Football Ball - Haiku

Exclusive designs
It's round and easy to kick
Into the net, *goal*.

Phil Wake (14)
Ansford School, Castle Cary

Shiny Red Balloon - Haiku

Shiny red balloon,
Soaring up into the sky,
Where will it end up?

Danny Ayres (14)
Ansford School, Castle Cary

The British Empire - Haiku

As the Empire fell
We had nothing left to do
So we tried again.

Nathan Gibbs (13)
Ansford School, Castle Cary

Rugby - Haiku

The coin flip is made,
The kick-off has been taken,
Try scored, what a game.

Will Chandler (13)
Ansford School, Castle Cary

Fireworks

Green, red, gold sparkles in the sky
Zoom, boom, whish, whoosh
Into the firework slosh
Shoots up into the sky
Explodes like a puffer fish
Children run to the window with excitement.

Gerard McQuade (14)
Ashcraig School, Glasgow

Different

When I think of being *different*
I think of being sad - lonely, excluded and depressed -
Why does my life have to be so bad?

I like living in this neighbourhood.
I wave to everyone I meet
But instead they give me really weird looks
As I walk across the street.

School isn't any fun
It's like a living hell.
Every time I hear the bell ring I end up feeling glum.

I don't really care for a uniform,
I don't want to *blend in with a crowd,*
I only want to be me - to really make a statement -
To really stand out!

Mum called the office today.
The headmaster replied, 'There's nothing we can do.'
But I know for a fact that is certainly not true!

I feel as though I'm under a microscope.
I feel shut away forever,
Being judged on how I *act*, *say* and *do* -
I really can't cope!

Who cares about being *different*?
Will you appreciate?
Will you continue to isolate?
Will you turn away from me?

Kirk Johnstone (18)
Ashcraig School, Glasgow

13

The Depths Of Our Lives

The ripples disperse over our sunken past
Silence
Breathe it in
Fresh air.
A fresh start
Grasp it with both hands, don't let go.
Our chance is nigh
What's done is done.
We can make a future
We are the future.
Walk away from the depths that enchant us
Build a new lake
Make a new past
Let the water take us
Let the wind guide us
Let the passion in our hearts run free.

Megan Pinches (17)
Bede Sixth Form College, Stockton-on-Tees

Screaming Out Loud

Whether to scream out in response to my mother's cries,
I lay there helplessly under the rubble.
My leg was trapped and trickling blood . . .

My hands shook with fear as I held my breath
And tried to stay calm.

I heard crying in the distance,
Hoping for someone to rescue me,
I started screaming for help.
My heart was pounding and I was breathing hard.

Dust and dirt surrounded me, clogging up my throat.
It was very hard to breathe.

Hours later I was found.
I was relieved, but I can never forget that tragic day.

Keesha Todd (12)
Blyth Tynedale Middle School, Northumberland

14

Panic In Haiti

Whether to screech out in reply to my mother's trapped shrieks
I can hear people's distant screams
Its jaws were coming closer and closer
Crunching everything in its path.
Its red, beaming eyes looked right into my soul.
I heard a loud bang and then a screen of black washed over me.
I couldn't see anything.
All I could hear was frantic parents in the distance.
I heard a child, I thought about shouting but I couldn't speak.
Whether to shout and lose my life
Or not to shout and lose that little boy's life?
I decided to shout.
Thankfully someone came and got the boy out
But didn't see me.
I started screaming, it didn't work.
Rubble cascaded down on top of the wreckage I was under.
Dust and dirt clung to my throat
Preventing me from sharing my thoughts and emotions with others.
Blood seeped through the gaps above me,
I started to lose consciousness . . .

As I lose hope
I hear voices crying out to me
Protection is coming
A ray of hope flickers in my mind.

Vivid memories of that treacherous day still echo in my mind.
Turmoil haunts me still as I wonder, *could I have done better?*
My thoughts are overcast by powerful memories
Which leave me paralysed by the fury of the storm.

Courtney Turner (11)
Blyth Tynedale Middle School, Northumberland

15

New Boy

As I walk along the street
A new boy is who I meet.
He asks me what I want to be,
I respond, 'I want to be free.'

I tell him about William Blake,
He tells me that it must be fake.
I tell him that I'm home-schooled,
He tells me that must be cool.

He has a little baby sister,
But he really missed her,
And now I am distracted
Because of the way he acted.

He has a lot of strange dreams,
But what can they really mean?
Is there something wrong or right?
There may be, there might.

I hope his baby sister's well,
If she's not, I hope Skellig will cast a spell.
The little baby is in bed,
I wonder what's inside her head?

His friend thinks that I am mad
And that makes me really sad.
Why do they think this about me?
I don't know, let's ask and see.

As I walk along the street
A new boy is who I meet.

Carla Downey (11)
Blyth Tynedale Middle School, Northumberland

16

Trapped!

My knees are shaking, my heart is beating
Nowhere to move, I'm trapped.

Bricks falling all around me
People shouting my name
I can't get my words out
Stuck under all the rubble
I'm trapped!

If I move I will die.
Babies crying in the distance
I'm trapped!

Lying motionless, all alone
Destruction all around
Tears streaming down my face
Dust clogging my throat
I'm trapped.

The hope of getting out is slowly fading . . .

Just as I think I am taking my last breath
I see the light
My father shifts bricks above my head
Through the cloud of thick ash
I can see him with my mother and brother
They are safe
I was so close to my grave.
I have survived . . .
Only just!

Kelsie Thompson (12)
Blyth Tynedale Middle School, Northumberland

17

Hope

Death's cape of darkness hung over the city
Shading every house and building.
The people of Haiti shrieked and screamed
At the horror of the monster's roar.
Hospitals tumbled, schools crumbled.

Bricks and stones fell from the skies above -
Crushing and suffocating.
They murdered the survivors who got out safely,
The jaws of the treacherous beast
Opened from under their feet.
Everyone who fell through was never seen again.
Bodies surrounded me,
Horrified from these sights I ran from
The main square to the edge of the city.
The monster attempted to kill me once more;
A building stumbled onto me and pinned me down with wood.
I couldn't move.
In panic I yelped for help.
All that was left was faint hope.
I yelled, shouted and screamed,
No reply for hours
Until finally a voice came from a crack
In the top half of the crumbled building.
'Is there anyone alive down there?'
I shouted, 'Yes!'
Hope had been restored.

Jack Richardson (11)
Blyth Tynedale Middle School, Northumberland

Earthquake In Haiti

It was the 10th January 2010.
I sat in my living room and settled down
To my usual night in front of the TV.
What followed was out of this world.
My curtains tore back and the windows blew open
With severe force.
I was horrified but remained focused
On the events taking place before my very eyes.
The door began to creak,
Opening the door and then closing,
Causing a horrendous banging noise
As loud as a bomb exploding.
I could hear the roof tiles
Being blown from the roof,
The swirling wind carried them for miles.
My memorable bookcase flung from
One side of the room to the other,
Smashing into several bits.
Toys began to play due to the force that
The earthquake implied through the house.
I was almost deafened by the noise of cutlery
Clanking into one another in the kitchen.
I sat hunched in the corner of my living room,
I shivered and felt alone gazing into the outside world,
Waiting and wondering if my family was safe
And when this nightmare would come to an end.

Kofi Park (11)
Blyth Tynedale Middle School, Northumberland

Stunned By An Angel Of Death

I watch stunned,
As the Angel of Death,
Spreads her large, painful cloak of darkness,
Over the city as it strikes.

The sky is suddenly overcast and grey,
Dust clogs my mouth as I cry,
The monster's anger gets worse,
It rumbles the city and everything becomes broken.

I can hear my mother's shrieking close by,
But in my mind distant,
I know I am travelling from the world of the living,
But then, I start to regain conciousness.

I manage to look up - I'm horrified
The Angel of Death has destroyed everything,
Buildings are nothing now but rubble and wood,
The monster has won its prize,
People lay around me,
Dead.

My mother then picks me up in her arms,
She tells me it's over at last; she tells me I'm safe,
Relief, I am overwhelmed
I shall never forgive that Devil
For taking the lives of people I love,
But I'm grateful to be here and alive.

Louise Beldon (12)
Blyth Tynedale Middle School, Northumberland

Underneath The Sheets Of Rubble And Dust

The Devil of death is here and winning the battle for my life,
As I shout for help under the sheets of rubble and glass.
He's getting stronger and more powerful,
I can't fight him any longer.

His aggression is affecting people.
Who should I shout for?
A friend or family? Or are they dead?
Maybe a stranger is my only saviour.

He is powerful and demanding.
You can feel him running along the ground
Causing vibrations.
His mouth opens like a black funnel and death occurs.
Thousands fall into his treacherous trap.

I survive it and I feel delighted.
After three hours of constant fury
I hear my father shouting and screaming my name.
I am scared to shout back in reply
In case I inhale the dust and it causes an infection.

Suddenly he stops.
Everyone searches for their loved ones.
I find my parents underneath a bus.
We are relieved that we are winners.

Courtney Heslop (12)
Blyth Tynedale Middle School, Northumberland

Summer Wind

The trees swayed smoothly
In the summer breeze.
The green grass glowed in the golden sun
As bushes waved in the warm, smooth, summer wind.
I walked through the dandelion fields
As they danced
In the whispering summer wind.

Ross Graham (11)
Blyth Tynedale Middle School, Northumberland

21

Running Away

I dodged the sheet of metal
That he threw at me,
The sounds of screaming echoed in my head,
My leg throbbed and seeped blood.
The earthquake still shook with rage
Causing demolition everywhere around me.

My hands shook with fear as he climbed
Over the building, crushing them all.
The cut in my leg, it filled with dirt
But I couldn't think about my leg
When there were children dead at this very moment.

Screaming filled the air around me,
My head filled with doubt as the rubble
Fell from the buildings as they cracked and creaked.
He was shaking in fury,
He whistled in anger.

I ran for ages, watching behind me
In case he was following me.
I ran into my mam, we huddled together
As I wept tears continuously.

Abbey McKay
Blyth Tynedale Middle School, Northumberland

Paralysed

I crawled along the blood-soaked floor,
A horrible stench lingered in the air around me.

As I lay shivering, a cold chill ran down my spine.
I couldn't move, I was in tremendous pain.
I kept telling myself I would find my parents soon.

As I lay there thinking to myself,
My father crawled out of a pile of rubble and dust.
I knew I would be alright.

Lee McShane (11)
Blyth Tynedale Middle School, Northumberland

Faint Hope

I lie and wait as fear shivers through my body.
The jaws open and I become more terrified.
I hear my mother's cries and shrieks.
Blood trickles down my leg,
A hint of light filters through a crack in the rubble.

In the distance, echoes of crying and shouting can be heard.
Dust and dirt from the relentless shake
Clogs up my throat.
Without warning, another shake occurs.
I want to cry, or should I keep silent?

As I'm tossed, I begin to cry,
In sore distress I shriek with fright.
I curl up in a ball in hope for safety.
Suddenly I hear voices, I begin to shout.

Voices calling back to me, I start to see light.
They hear my cry suddenly, then rocks crash around me,
But no need to fear, they have found me.
Soon I am out and I see the sun once more,
And I am back in my mother's arms again and
Taken to shelter for food and water.

Jessica Waugh (11)
Blyth Tynedale Middle School, Northumberland

End Of My Life Is Near

The end of my life is nearly here
As I lie upon this dusted air.

I can feel it killing me
But I find it hard to think of my own life
As the children around are dying.

I should yell, but the final bricks of my home
Are piling over my body.
I am worn out.
The bricks crash upon my chest
As I lay slowly dying.

This beast is in a vexed rage
Thrashing through our empty streets.

Just as I am taking my last breaths
I see the light, it is blinding me.
I think I am dead
But then suddenly I see a face
Reaching towards me . . .

I am relieved to see my father's arm
Dragging me out of the dusty rubble.

Danielle Agnew (12)
Blyth Tynedale Middle School, Northumberland

Tangled Shrieks

The earthquake that has just stricken the Earth
Without any warning
Is still roaring nearby, just waiting to pounce
Through the cracks of the pavement over my head
The world flashes before my eyes

I wonder if I should yelp out
Or keep quiet in my terror
As I hear my mother's tangled shrieks of fury
I feel suffocated more and more each moment
As the dust and dirt of the rubble collapses on my face

As the treacherous rocks
Are lifted from my weak body
I sigh a sigh of relief
As my body is lifted from under the rubble
And into the light

I breathe the air and see the light
Then realise that I am one of many survivors to be alive
My mother holds me and tells me softly,
'You're safe now, there is no need to worry.'

Hannah Eastman (11)
Blyth Tynedale Middle School, Northumberland

Skellig Poem

Sitting in a corner all alone,
With crackling, flaky bones,
I share a room with dust and spiders
And bluebottles in my hair.

I have no family,
I have no friends,
Michael is like my family.
Whereas Mina, she is wonderful
And is a ray of sun.

Why do people look and stare
Whilst I try to move?
All I am is an angel with wings,
I need somebody to love.

Let me find my family,
Let me find a home,
It is not fair on Michael and Mina
Having to feed me night and day,
When they also have an interesting life
To live up to just as well as me.

Shannon Lynch (11)
Blyth Tynedale Middle School, Northumberland

Salvation

As I lay there paralysed with pain and fear,
Tears escaped my eyes.
My whole family had been taken from me.
Did I really deserve all this, did we deserve this?
All possible hope had been taken away from me;
The relentless earthquake had taken down all this city was worth!
A sudden cry made the rocks around me quiver
And shout back, but dust clogged my throat.
The ground around me shook again,
Panic flooded over me from top to bottom
And everything was rocking backwards and forwards.
I lay there trying to let the dust and rocks kill me bit by bit.
Slowly, the cries kept getting louder and louder.
Suddenly light flooded my surroundings.
Cries gone, the rubble gone, I was dying,
But then I was falling back, back into the rubble-filled heap.
A face appeared above me, 'You're OK, son, it's all over!'
I lay on the stretcher and wondered where my family was.
Did my mum risk her life to protect me?
Feelings of relief mixed with guilt stung me.

Reece McLoughlin (12)
Blyth Tynedale Middle School, Northumberland

Hope For Haiti

As I watched, the ground cracked open
Like the jaws of Hell.
People screamed and ran for their lives,
Buildings collapsed all around me.
He was destroying everything: the Devil.

Blood spurted from my leg, but nobody helped me.
My thoughts were dark and black,
The pain was horrible, I was going to die.
I could hear the distant cries of other people like me, trapped.
A sudden aftershock, more rubble from buildings landed on me,
I was suffocating.
He let out a third roar of terror,
More and more buildings destroyed.
Everything gone.

A beam of light, there was hope for me.
More light shone through the cracks,
It blinded me as I was lifted into the air.
I was saved.
We had beaten the Devil and I was alive.

Luke Freeman (12)
Blyth Tynedale Middle School, Northumberland

Survival

Earthquake tastes like dust attacking and choking people
With its terrible cloud of death.
It passes through the city, taking out everything in its path,
Wrathful and terrifying, roaring as in battle with fury.

Death is flowing towards me, breaking my protection;
I'm cowering in panic.
The monster is groaning, it wants more,
People call out for help but no one is there to help them.

I dodge the stone rocks which are soaring and flying with rage
Across the valley, people are crying and dying,
Destruction is all around me.

People praying, hoping to survive, losing faith,
The gates of Hell have opened.
They think all hope is lost. Do they deserve all this?

We all hope this will stop soon.
We hope we will get help soon, with shelter and food,
And see the light again,
But we cannot bring back the people we have lost!

Laurence Joseph (12)
Blyth Tynedale Middle School, Northumberland

29

Skellig

As I sit here all alone
I have no cosy home
I sit here with moans and groans
With weak, sore and flaky bones

I feed on flies and spiders
No longer lives Ernie Myers
I used to live on 27 and 53
But now there's not even that for me

Nobody is here to forgive
So why do I even live?
I have long hair and dusty clothes
All I hear is birds and crows

My wing in my back all curled and crushed
In this corner I feel all mushed
I wish I was like an owl
All wild and free
But I can't do that
Because I'm me!

Lisa Ferrow (12)
Blyth Tynedale Middle School, Northumberland

When The Wind Blows

When the wind blows, the trees whistle and dance
To the soothing sound of rustling leaves.
The gentle wind touches your cold face.
Oh no, it's starting to rain.
Lightning, thunder, it's so powerful.
You can hardly see in front of you.
As terrible as a tiger, it's so dark and dangerous.
It's unstoppable, it's uncontrollable.
Clouds are coming from over the hills,
Racing past each other,
They have a dark grey colour.
Now the storm is settling down, the wind is blowing gently.
All the leaves are scattered to the ground,
But they are not alone.
The rain has soaked the ground and all around
Are puddles up to your middle.
The clouds are starting to go away.
Hip hip hooray!

Chloe Watson (13)
Blyth Tynedale Middle School, Northumberland

Earthquake In Haiti

Animals running from the gates of Hell, trying to survive,
Blood trickling from the buildings that have tumbled down,
Babies and children crying for their mums and dads,
Rescuers searching for people who are lost,
Terrible smell of gas chambers leaking,
And cars and buildings exploding.
Searching for a way to survive,
Wondering if it was my time to die.
Would I fall to Hell or would I manage to live?
Just as all hope is lost for me,
My mum and dad find me and my brother,
We join medics from afar coming to save injured people.

Kyle Clifton (11)
Blyth Tynedale Middle School, Northumberland

31

Rubble All Around Me

I was in my home, a loud boom roared,
A moment later furniture was sliding down the room.
I could feel his fury as he tore apart my house with anger
And threw bricks at me.
Dust trapped my throat.

I climbed through the rubble, heading for the front door.
His jaws opened with force as he destroyed my street.
Buildings were collapsing one by one,
I shook with fear.
A moment later a rock came from above
Crashing down on my leg.
Blood seeped as I lay in the rubble, hoping for help.

I could see beams of light in the distance.
I yelped for help desperately, more and more light came in.
I watched with hope.
I was stunned as I saw a face through the rubble.
I was safe, it was over.

Kyle Castelow (12)
Blyth Tynedale Middle School, Northumberland

Trapped In A Cage!

They're trapped inside a cage,
They don't know if they're going to live or die.
The monster is incessant,
He won't stop until he gets them all!

A girl cries in horror, she needs help.
We need to get to her.
Now he has gone, they're struggling forward in life.
No parents, no food or drink.

At last they are safe but they need help.
They can live their life in peace.
We're lucky to have what we have got.
Please help Haiti, they need us!

Shannen Butterfield (12)
Blyth Tynedale Middle School, Northumberland

32

Summer Angel

One summer's day I was blessed
When an angel laid his hand upon my chest
My heart went *thud*
I did not treat the angel the way I should

His heart and soul were in vain
He helped me when I was in pain
I am the one to blame
For this, a great summer shame

I wish he would return
As I will be stern
When I give him my apology
As the sun sets past the sea

He came without a smile
I was in great denial
Then a smile came to his face
I looked closely at his amazing grace.

Lewis Sayers (12)
Blyth Tynedale Middle School, Northumberland

Haiti In Distress

I try to move but can't,
The ground is shaking, buildings collapsing.
The mouth opened wide, it starts swallowing lives.
One moment my mam is here; next she is gone!
I feel as if I'm frozen, I can't move, I'm in shock.
I stare in panic and disbelief.
I can't believe what has just happened
To others, to me - the people of Haiti.

Later, without warning, people start pushing.
Family, friends, strangers, fighting for food and water.
I'm knocked to the ground! The panic has begun!
I run for cover and shelter.
Hope just starts to fade away!

Ross Miller (12)
Blyth Tynedale Middle School, Northumberland

33

Haiti Needs Help

In the dark, gloomy hovel,
Terrified, I shook with terror,
My heart pounding as sheets of glass
Came crashing around me.

I could hear the screaming for help
By the people,
Then without warning, the monster's jaws
Demolished everything in its path.

I could hear my mother's cries for help echoing,
Blood trickled down the door posts
Which were now crashed to one side.

To my amazement I escaped
With only a broken arm.
Finally first aid came to my rescue
For the first time.

Ainsley Foster (12)
Blyth Tynedale Middle School, Northumberland

When The Wind Blows

At midday one afternoon,
The wind woke with a start.
It howled and roared like a tiger in a cage
And whistled through the tall trees.
It blew all the flowers aside
And destroyed the entire town.

It travelled through the town,
As strong as an ox,
And knocked all the children to the ground.
It growled at anything in its path.
If you stood in its way, it would blow you away.
Then it calmed to a nice gentle breeze,
And then suddenly it stopped.

Margaret Short (11)
Blyth Tynedale Middle School, Northumberland

34

Haiti - Lost Under The Rubble

Trapped, scared and confused,
I watch dust fall, I hear screams of terror and fear.
Flashes of grey, light and blackness fill this place,
A place that was once happy and colourful,
Now lays lost under the rubble,
Lost as an abandoned world.

It's hard to breathe; warm dust
Clings to my throat and makes me cough.
I wish to see the sunlight and breathe fresh air.
I crawl along the dusty floor pushing rubble;
It doesn't move.
The sharpness of the rubble cuts my leg
And blood gushes.
I begin to lose hope but try once more to push ahead,
Terrified, but determined to see sunlight again.

Georgia Livingstone (12)
Blyth Tynedale Middle School, Northumberland

Survival

The earthquake's rumble shook the Earth
Then the terror began.
It almost deafened me.
Taken to a nearby shelter.
The monster's jaws opened wide and devoured the building
Like it was for his breakfast.
The rains of horror continuously destroyed
Buildings, houses and lives.
To my horror, the mountainous waves
Terrorised our villages.
To my amazement I escaped with only minor injuries.
Compared to others, how could I complain?

Christopher McGlen (12)
Blyth Tynedale Middle School, Northumberland

35

Ruins Of My Life

The crumbling houses tremble with fear
A monster has descended, its carnage costs dear.

I lie in the ruins which once were my life
My house, my career, my children, my wife.

Bricks start to shift, I've no strength to yell
My home has become my own living hell.

I lie in the ruins of my own despair
The fabric of life just seems so unfair.

The sounds of digging, my hope is restored
A glimpse of the heavens, I pray to the Lord.

Heather Nelson (12)
Blyth Tynedale Middle School, Northumberland

The Bully

I run into the toilets, trying to hide
She said it wouldn't hurt - she lied, she lied!
She tries to torment me from behind the door,
She somehow gets in, pushes me on the floor.
The pain, the pain all over again.
Oh please, dear Lord, oh please let it end!
After a moment or two, she gets bored and walks out,
So now I am left here, unable to shout.
A few hours later I get up and walk home,
But there she waits, her heart made of stone.
So I build up the courage, try to walk right past,
But she stops me dead still so I dare to ask,
'Why do you bully me so?' I said it despite my fears,
But to my surprise, she burst into tears.
'I just didn't know how I'd hurt you so,
But your mother told me and then I felt low.'
I thought about her apology, long and hard,
I eventually forgave her and we've never been apart!

Jorjia Wintersgill (11)
Chilton Cantelo School, Yeovil

Poetry, A History

I'll start at the very beginning
When poetry first began
The oldest tellers of poetry are Neanderthal Man.
Now we move forward to 800BC
To Homer, the Iliad and the Odyssey.
Let's go closer to the present day
To Greece, to a poetic play
Depicting battles and war
Very interesting, I'm sure.
In Tudor times there lived a great man
Shakespeare was his name, William.
He wrote plays about love, about tragedy too
His words extend between me and you.
But closer to home, the Victorian age
To Keats, Wordsworth and Stevenson (strange)
Lonely clouds and a railway carriage
And daffodils (savage).
And now let's go to the present day
To Carol Ann Duffy, the poet laureate.
Today's poetry is immediate.
Whatever form poetry is in
Remember this, it will always win
Because poetry is stronger than ordinary words
So I hope you've paid attention to what you've just heard.

Fintan Munnery (11)
Chilton Cantelo School, Yeovil

37

Tears

Tears run down my flaming cheeks,
Why, oh why is it me?
So what? I'm different, it's not my fault.
Why, oh why can't they see?

Then tomorrow at school I'll have to face them again,
I'll need to find somewhere to hide,
But they'll find me then chase me, shove me and kick me,
They don't know how much they hurt me inside.

I wish I could tell someone, oh how I wish,
But telling would just make things worse.
I'll have to deal with this on my own,
It feels like my life is a curse.

I head over to my window, I open it wide,
The breeze is harsh and cold.
I try to summon the courage to do what I'm thinking
But no, there's more of my story to be told.

Isabella Humphreys (12)
Chilton Cantelo School, Yeovil

Untitled

With fur as fluffy as
The feathers in my pillow
And with ears as floppy
As banana skins
The rabbit hopped along
With the wind whistling
Through his fur, his ears
Flapping like kites in the
Roaring wind and his
Dark red eyes glistening
In the light.

Marcus Pratt (12)
Chilton Cantelo School, Yeovil

38

My Friendship Poem

We can get in fights
And I can get annoying
But we can't let that get in the way,

For our friendship is rich
And our friendship is pure,
And we will never give that away.

We've been friends for a while,
Having fun on the way
And enjoying every second
Of every day,

So we won't let that fade
After one little fight,
And we need each other
Day and night.

Hayley Symonds (12)
Chilton Cantelo School, Yeovil

Slaves To These Sounds

Music makes the world go round,
Perks you up, yet
Can bring you down
But still we listen,
Slaves to these sounds,
Either pop or rock,
Metal or hip hop,
Whichever your favourite
You listen, you love,
Slaves to these sounds,
Arguments caused or solved
Over good or bad, best or worst,
Amazing how we are
Slaves to these sounds.

Conor Trapnell (15)
Chilton Cantelo School, Yeovil

My Poem To My Great Grandfather

Born in World War I
Crying or those falling dead in war
Fighting in World War II
He bled
For us to sleep in bed
Not in a shed
Or a fiery shed burnt by a bomb
Those stories he said to me
With the heat on his head from the sun
Travelling across the sea
To D-Day trenches
Look back to when we sat on benches
I wish you will remember me
Till the eyes lose down as we fall.

James Hayton (12)
Chilton Cantelo School, Yeovil

40

The Battlefield

As I sit by myself, alone and shamed,
Terrified and cold, for the sins I was blamed.
My heart beats strongly, coming out of my chest,
I know this was brought upon me so I could pass this test.
The screams I hear, the shouts I dread,
Walking across the battlefield, the soldiers I led.
The guns and grenades, the smoke and the sound,
In our heads we were lost and couldn't be found.
Full of hate and disloyalty I watch the soldiers kill,
Watching friends pass away, with dread I fill.
As I drop my gun I hear lots of loud talk,
I walk across the battlefield, I take my last walk.
I stand between the battle for and against,
Whispers and words they tell you the best.
Trying to stand firm, withered with smoke,
The bullet hits me hard, in my blood I soak.
It powers through my chest, my lungs and my blood,
The pain hits me hard like a powerful flood.
The look on their faces, the blankness of mind,
The bullet sinks deep, no one can ever find.
Trying to compose, trying to stay strong,
The pain and the tears I've coped too long.
I breathe in and out, my lungs close in,
My heart feels heavy and tight is my skin.
I see the faces of my friends, my fellow believers,
The thoughts pass my mind as I stare at the grievers.
Time to say goodbye, farewell and goodnight,
Like they say, at the end of the tunnel I saw the white light.
Watching the mournful, the counting of death,
I fell across the dirt as I took my last breath.

Lois Birkinshaw (13)
Druridge Bay Middle School, Northumberland

My Sister's Tantrum

Dare you read this page
Because it is full of rage.
My little sister has the loud screams.
She runs around kicking Dad as it seems.
She throws cups at the wall,
How do my parents put up with it all?
She screams loud, her voice bellows,
She even smashes my cello.
She beats the floor good and hard,
She rips paper and our holiday cards.
She never stops, it's a nightmare,
All of this madness I just can't bear.
It never stops, she can go on all day,
All this madness to get her own way.
After that she gets sent to her room,
When she does it again it could be my doom.

Harry Ferranti Donavellas (13)
Fairmead Special School, Yeovil

My Anger

My head is burning up
About to explode like a firework
Red face like a ball of fire
Neck and throat feel tighter

And I get a tummy ache
Like an erupting volcano
Lava spilling out of my eyes
I can't stop this feeling
However hard I try

I get angrier now
And my muscles
And I get tense.
Anger gets tense.

Jason Hathway (14)
Fairmead Special School, Yeovil

42

My Face

Skin as pale as yoghurt
And hair like straw

Mousey-brown hair
Lips like red pepper

And bendy glasses
Like people who own free bus passes

My little nose
Long like a hose

And eyes like marbles
With 14 years of stories to tell.

Luke Harris (13)
Fairmead Special School, Yeovil

My Face

My hair is like a teddy bear
My white face is like a pear
I'm going to a fair
Bright blue eyes
Like a sea
See my rosy-posy-red cheeks
My eyebrows are like a tree in a breeze.

Jayke Bugler (14)
Fairmead Special School, Yeovil

Cars Of The World

Americans have their muscle cars,
The Japanese have their sports cars
And Germans have their big, heavy, four wheel drives.
The French have their Peugeots
But sadly, the British have their crummy hatchbacks
That break down within 100 yards.

Ben Griffiths (13)
Fairmead Special School, Yeovil

43

My Anger

Brain bubbling like a kettle
Overheating and sweating
Like an engine growling
Like a wolf's stomach
Bubbling like a bubble bath
Butterflies flutter in my tummy
And my ears steam like a furnace.

Morgan Axford (14)
Fairmead Special School, Yeovil

My Anger

When I get angry I punch a pillow sometimes.
Sometimes when I'm angry, my cheeks are rosy and hot.
When I get angry I swear at my friends or mum.
When I sometimes get angry,
My eyebrows go up and my head shakes.

Macauley England (12)
Fairmead Special School, Yeovil

My Angry Body

My mouth is red like cherries
My teeth grit together
Fists are tight
Stamping feet.

Liam Harrisson (14)
Fairmead Special School, Yeovil

44

The Future Is A Question

The future is a question,
Asked today and yesterday.
But future in my mind,
Is just a simple sentence.

Maybe it has different creatures,
From all the different planets.
The different human beings,
Animals from today and tomorrow.

In future, no one dies,
And ancient animals return.
Everyone is peaceful,
You're not surprised to see an alien.

The transportation would be different,
Flying cars across the streets.
Massive ships soar through the universe,
Time machines transport to past.

Anyway, until the time machine is invented
I can't know the real truth.
But, still my imagination,
Wouldn't stop a minute!

Dominyka Stanaityt (12)
Friary Grange School, Lichfield

The Future

Walking through the street,
Walking to my own beat,
Everywhere flying cars,
And drunk people in cyber bars,
People watching TV channels,
Living in houses with solar panels,
A robot walking a pet dog,
And a rocket flying to Mars in a fog,
This is what the future will be like.

Josh Tomlinson (11)
Friary Grange School, Lichfield

45

What Is Happening?

We have made
Robots, flying cars
Hover boards and zero-gravity rooms
What is there?
There is:
Less
Poaching, violence
Less
Thoughtless killing
But . . .
There is a glitch
The world is coming to an end
We are still spinning but very, very slowly
All at once very hot then
Totally freezing cold
We . . . We . . .
Have stopped
What can we do?
The Earth is now dead!
We will all die!
One last world.

Jordon Harley (11)
Friary Grange School, Lichfield

The Future

Flying cars are all around.
Robots are normal now.
Guns are still firing.
But now there are lasers.
People keep on hiring.
People keep on making games.
But each now have different aims.
For all the ages in a range.

Harvey Smith (12)
Friary Grange School, Lichfield

46

Future Voices

The future is not the past
The past has gone
The future's coming
The future is life to come
People, plants and animals
Have all got future voices.

Future voices, echo, echo, echo
Future voices fly
You have that sense
You have that feeling
There's something in the air
Echo, echo, future voices.

Future voices are coming
It may be tomorrow
In a year or a month
Seeping through the present
Whispering in your ear are
Future voices.

Helena Cook (12)
Friary Grange School, Lichfield

Fused

One person rules the world,
Our whole lives will be curled,
More rules will be made,
More money will be paid,
More thieves around,
A pencil costs a hundred pounds,
A cure for cancer,
A robot dancer,
Too much electricity being used,
This world is gonna fuse,
The world will die,
And the question is why?

Lauren Starkey (12)
Friary Grange School, Lichfield

Humans Of 2105

Up into space, to the stars,
To the moon and Mars.
While people live and sleep,
Passenger spacecraft meet.

10,000,000 people on the moon,
Everyone humming a happy tune,
Under a man-made atmosphere,
And now, no one lives in fear.

10,000,000 people on Mars,
Everyone has flying cars,
All people live in peace,
With very
Big
Alien
Geese!

Henry Robinson (12)
Friary Grange School, Lichfield

Possible

Things we think now that couldn't exist,
People flying around in flying cars,
People living up on Mars,
Robots doing all your needs,
People seeing talking trees,
People will be flying instead of walking,
Everything will be possible as it's in the future,
Disappearing in magic tricks,
Time can stop and living forever,
All will be possible a few decades on.

Lizzie Hosier (12)
Friary Grange School, Lichfield

The Day The Earth Stood Still

The Earth is still,
The sky is static,
The moon keeps moving,
It can't stop,
The sun burns down,
Stronger than ever,
It hurts,
It burns,
We all die,
The Earth dies with us.

James Burns (12)
Friary Grange School, Lichfield

Robot Police

Robot policemen patrolling the street
In flying cruisers looking for Scabby Pete.
Robot people with metal jumping and bouncing to the beat.
Whatever, you didn't lose me
Otherwise, there goes technology.
So bounce to the beat and move your feet
And help me find Scabby Pete.

Declan Hanks (12)
Friary Grange School, Lichfield

Uprising

People get what they desired
Gordon Brown is finally fired.
People pleased and people drinking,
The people's government power is shrinking
Cherishing food and super-sizing
A toast to the people's uprising.

Jacob Jones (12)
Friary Grange School, Lichfield

Shove Ower Rabbie

Heh Rabbie! Will ye stop
Addressing yon haggis till you drop?
Rambling like yer red, red rose
Sowping red wine up your nose.

Yer moose is deed in oor eyes
Yer farmer tells a lot of lies
Aboot time spent
Chasing thon wee moose,
That ran hoose tae field and field tae hoose.

Tam O'Shanter's had his day
Old Meg's tail has gone away
To string auld Chopin's violin
Or to the bed for Tam's witch tae sleep in.

Should your acquaintance be forgot
Your poems to be forgotten not.
You were a legend in your day
But your message now is old and grey.

Go take a cup o' kindness for the sake of Old Lang Syne.
Rest yer heed, put up your feet
Squeeze ower and make some room
For us weans,
Wi new blood, new words and new sayings
Are catching up behind . . .

**Christopher Kelly, Melissa Stafford, Stephen Coia,
Adam Melville, Natalie Spence, Craigjohn Clark (16),
Euan Marshall & David Harvey**
Glencryan School, Glasgow

My Positive Poem

Your're the music on my CD,
You're the chocolate that I eat,
You're the films that I watch
And you're the bedroom that I keep neat.

You're the books that I read,
You're the money which I get,
You're the TV that I watch,
And you're my nice jewellery set.

You're the flowers that I have,
You're the sea at the side
You're the sun in the sky
And you're the bike that I ride.

Anisa Khaliq (12)
Hall Green Secondary School, Birmingham

My Barcelona FC Poem!

Barcelona have Messi
Messi scores great goals!
He is the best!

Barcelona have Iniesta
Iniesta, great crosser!
Scores great goals!

Barcelona have Pique
Signed from great rivals Man United
Great defender!

That's it from Barcelona
They are great!
Messi is great!

Aaron Bansel (12)
Hall Green Secondary School, Birmingham

51

My Dad Poem

My dad is the best
I love my dad
My dad looks after me
My dad buys me things

My dad takes care of me
My dad is there for me
My dad always loves me

My dad buys me everything
My dad cares about me
My dad protects me
My dad is the best in the world.

Raheel Mohammed (12)
Hall Green Secondary School, Birmingham

Word Party

Long words stretch their voices out
Short words do not scream and shout
Sneaky words like to play dares
Other words go to their pairs
Bold words stick out in the groups
Old words won't go for the hoops
Note words speak like they are put
Coal words go and spit out soot
Physical words kick and punch
Hungry words go for their lunch
Fashion words like to make up poses

Snap . . . the dictionary closes.

Suzy Haines (12)
Hampton Community College, Hampton

52

Lover

Hatred in absence, passion in presence
My soul leaps when near, skips when drawn apart
Peace surrounding, still I fall cold and dense
Love found who I was and captured my heart

Reminiscence of thoughts I know we share
Struck with wonder at mention of your name
Filled with joy as I imagine you there
As long as I'm here I'll love you the same

At times desire is lost, not soon regained
Not reflection of the mind inside
What is portrayed outward rends me insane
Together alive, when parted it died

Had it figured out, thoughts now lost to me
Just reveal yourself and set my heart free.

Rebecca-Ashley Clark (14)
Holyrood Community School, Chard

Tears

Look in the mirror,
What do you see?
I see a scared little girl
Staring back at me.
The tears in her eyes
Now fall to the floor,
Leaking salted pain,
Crying out no more.

Emily Davis (13)
Holyrood Community School, Chard

The Real Me

Only the deaf can hear me *scream.*
Only the blind can see me *cry.*
Only the numb can feel my *pain.*
So nobody knows the *real me.*

Mollie Waring (13)
Holyrood Community School, Chard

A Girl Called Evan

Being different's never good enough
A close call, non-conformist
She saw the world in shades of grey
Not black and white or gold
they'd promised.

In place of her, a boy arrived
Soft-spoken, faint of heart
As Evan he addressed himself
And soon found he could not
depart.

Now, little Evan is this girl
Just carefully disguised;
The product of a world from which
She felt she had to shrink
and hide.

His life's a lie
One twisted tale
Once beautiful
Now not quite male.

A vanity which treads thin ice
Androgyny will now suffice.

Gillian Hazel (16)
Larkhall Academy, Larkhall

54

The Scottish Snow

In Scotland it hardly ever snows
It usually just rains
It is a pain, I must complain
That the frost just ever grows

This year was quite different
Suddenly snow fell!
In every street, in every home
The children felt just swell

As for the oldies, it was otherwise
The snow was cold and slippy -
Which they totally despise

Now the snow has landed
The kids come out to play
Throwing snowballs, playing games
An old guy runs away

A few weeks have gone by
The snow is getting boring
Many cars will not start
You can hear the engines roaring.

Niamh Cork (12)
Larkhall Academy, Larkhall

Promises

Towering body walking past,
Stroking my hair as it went,
The ghost of the enclosure
Watching life walk away
Rattling, scratching, rustling, stomping,
So many things which I don't care about,
So many things I do,
So many things you have to tell me,
The answers to my questions I don't understand.
The main question incomplete,
Leaving us in mayhem.
You told me to be patient,
You told me to be fine,
You told me to be the best I could be,
You told me to be kind.
Walking without a warning,
No signs I could see,
Only arguments to settle matters,
No sweet words said.
Picking up your future,
Smiling at your past,
The last time you will be seen in this graveyard
And the last time you will come and see me,
As you are given a new script
Your old character is forgotten.
Your haunting film, moved to the discount rack,
But still exists inside the shop.
Maybe it will be a hit again,
Or maybe it never was . . .

Georgia Todd
Marlborough College, Marlborough

56

Moms

Old tobacco, new books
Fill my head
As I glide downstairs.

She is in the kitchen,
My beautiful grandma,
Cooking her only dish: scrambled eggs.

Her golden hair, curled to perfection,
Light blue eyes mirroring mine,
Cream-coloured suit, matching heels and her pearl necklace.
Just because.

Windows wrap the kitchen,
Reflecting sun off the marble, wood and metal.
The back door is open,
Letting in the warm New Orleans air
And the winter-blue skies.

She puts my eggs on a plate,
Making sure I am ready for today,

Because I know she will take me to the park,
Feed the ducks
And protect me from all the scary ones.

This is what I try to remember.
I am lucky, as I remember.

Adelaide Goodyear
Marlborough College, Marlborough

Grand Jeff

On that soft, comfy chair, smoking his pipe,
Smiling, just smiling all day long.
His captivating voice drew me ever closer
As I listened to everything he said.

In a bungalow by the sea,
Fields surrounded us, with rounded hills,
Semicircles, one after another,
For miles on end.

The noise of the kettle, whistling away,
Never stopped.
Of course he'd still be in the chair,
He never got out of it for four years.

A few years later, reminiscing at the time
About a great man, both old and wise,
A man so nice, influential but kind.
Forever he will be remembered,
Always in my mind.

Charlie McKelrey
Marlborough College, Marlborough

Morning

The cold attacks me
Like a lion tearing up its prey,
As his teeth sink slowly in.
A truck breathes wearily
Whilst the sky looms above and beyond.
A grey monster.

Rain dances its way to the ground,
Landing in puddles
Which ripple and swirl.
Beside the chapel stands a tree,
Vast and unmoving,
Bare branches spread like claws.

Claudia Cox
Marlborough College, Marlborough

58

Overgrown Sprinter

I see his small stature,
His long, wavy hair bouncing,
Each strand an individual path, to an individual destination
With each stride,
One leg in front of another, such an easy task but
So long to perfect.
He brushes the long grass away,
With each crisp step.
As he reaches the top only he knows what lies ahead,
Towards the surrounding trees,
What is his vision?
The wind swirls and encloses him,
As I watch in amazement.
Then the gentle humming of a tractor
Disturbs the innocence of the peacefulness,
But leaves in his wake
The bliss of freshly cut,
Green, pure, newly-exposed grass.

Archie Turner
Marlborough College, Marlborough

Winter's Morn

Once again a drizzly start
To the chirpy town in deep Wiltshire.
Children played for hours on end,
With cars whizzing past on the Bath road.

Last year's plants shivering in the cold,
Waiting till spring's warm, happy days,
The grass swaying from side to side,
Kept in perfect condition.

At ten-past ten the clanging ceased
And the poor old chapel was left
As workers went and had their tea,
To get away from this miserable winter's day.

Tom Harris (15)
Marlborough College, Marlborough

Spring Not Yet Come

Clang of tools from the builder on the scaffolding,
Rumble of his van, left on beside him.
The cloudy cold makes all seem brighter,
Greener grass,
Redder bricks.
Light patter of raindrops creates
Quiet stillness.

Traffic rolls past quietly,
Icy wind blowing hair, moving branches,
The wall of God protects us.
Quiet breathing,
The rustle of movement,
Nothing else disturbs the peace.

The cold moves in like a blanket,
Rain envelops you,
No use trying to shelter,
You can't hide from the inevitable.

Jemima Weir
Marlborough College, Marlborough

February At Marlborough

The air is cold and crisp,
Wisps of steam lift from every breath.
The grass is damp and soft,
With the dew sitting on the tops of the blades.

The neighbouring road is alive with traffic,
But the rest of court was still and quiet.
The motionless grey sky was fitting
For the tranquillity of a February morning.

Occasionally the touch of a cold drop will strike you,
The chilliness in the air makes your goosebumps rise.
Wet and grimy are the stones on the path,
Sending a grim chill up your spine.

Ben Woodhouse
Marlborough College, Marlborough

60

Festival

Delicious crêpes, sweets, hot dogs
Flood with the typical festival smells.
Incredible colours at every stall.

Hiking through the weight of mud and grime,
Towing my sister behind, crying.
She whines for 'Mama',
Pinching and prodding my back and arm.

We progress slowly past gigglers, screamers, kissers, drunkards,
To the main destination, the major attraction: the rides.
Now I am towed around endless merry-go-rounds and swings,
Each with something better than the previous,
Flashier, brighter, faster or prettier.

Laden with balloons, striped sweet bags, stuffed teddies and toys
We make our way back slower to the car,
The buzz and excitement of the festival
Already far behind.

Jessamy Dibben
Marlborough College, Marlborough

Marlborough Springtime

Leaves blow in the whistling, chilly wind
Wafting the smell of today's lunch
Background noises echo around
As the early morning traffic engines
Stop for the traffic lights.
People non-existent in my mind
As I trudge down to the sweet
Scent of the rose garden.
Chapel, as always, standing tall.
I taste the bittersweetness of
The Marlborough springtime morning.

James McPherson
Marlborough College, Marlborough

61

Crush

A weight is crushing me.
Its infinite depth falls with the water.
Crazed light dazzles, blinds,
Piercing the silence of the woods all around.

A thought is crushing me.
Rustling through the trees.
Deeper, deeper,
Coming and going with stirring leaves.

A memory is crushing me.
Cool ether, shrouding my mind,
Pulls me back from the edge;
The water roar fades.

The silence is crushing me.
The empty, the nothing,
Fills my soul completely.
Where?

Michael Miller
Marlborough College, Marlborough

Sensual Morning

The cold, crisp wind, wet with the breeze.
Overcast but with no movement.
Silence but for the gentle sound of engines.
The steady *hum-drum* of traffic nearby,
With a background chant of children playing.
The grass is well kept, the ball in the middle.

The towering chapel doors of great iron and wood.
Hard rock, well polished, smooth, marks the edge.
Trees and fields head into the distance, peaceful.
Traffic, louder as cars fly by at breakneck speed.
Silence, a split-second then finally resumed by traffic.
The dense fresh air, invigorating to the skin.

Silence now but for the angle grinder in the distance,
The grass is soft underfoot; trees gently sway.
This morning was a sensual morn.

Alastair Dibden
Marlborough College, Marlborough

Blackberries

They stand out from the rest:
Purple and succulent.
When they ripen from a bright red,
It means another trip down the lane
With the bowls in hand, laughing.
My sister and I.
When she thinks I'm not looking,
She puts one more into her mouth.
The stains give her away.
I leave the high ones for her to reach
And I retreat to sit on the gate,
Ordering her around.
We collect until the bowls are full,
And return home with sticky hands
Every September.

Emily Hedges
Marlborough College, Marlborough

63

Allied Enemies

My squad are the worst, why?
Because they all hate each other, that's why
They hate and fight one another as if they were Nazis
The only one who can keep the peace between the men is me,
their sergeant
But no matter how much I maintain order within my squad
They still hate each other and they still fight
For you see, my squad first disliked each other
When they were training

It happened when they were practising shooting
at the enemy targets
One of them as a joke fired a bullet at one of them
Then they started doing it and eventually it broke out
into a fist fight between the four of them
Since then they have all hated one another's guts
I'm the one preventing them from killing each other.

But when we were scouting, I decided we should
rest for the night and I fell asleep
But when I woke up I found the men dead,
killed themselves by using their guns like clubs
When I gave word of what happened,
I was stripped of rank and discharged from the army
And when I leave, I wonder if the same thing
will happen to another new squad like mine,
and if things will turn out differently than mine.

Matthew Hutton (17)
Merkland School, Glasgow

Forsaken

Wind rushed against the window of an old house
That lay on the land far from the . . .
Other houses.
The empty rooms show the
Only people who had lived were gone now
In the house which is a ghostly and
Hollow shell of what it once was.

John Duffy (17)
Merkland School, Glasgow

The Lonely Cereus

The flowers start to raise their heads,
I can see all of this from my bed.
There's pink, yellow, red and blue ones,
Out in the garden there's tons and tons.
They follow the burning sun across the sky,
The one thing that I ask is, 'Why?'
They open up during the day.
If when the sun sets you go away,
Why can't you stay up at night?
Why go away with the light?
Please, please, can you stay
With me so we can play?
It's not my fault that I'm a Cereus.
So I'm asleep when you chuckle and fuss.
Please stay with me
Because I'm very lonely, you see.
It's too late now, I need to sleep,
I'll just have to keep trying
Good morning.

Kirsty Stewart (16)
Newcastle Bridges School, Newcastle upon Tyne

The Morgue

The cold corridors
Lit up by the small artificial lights
Beams of light-luminous rays ricochet across the walls.
Pure gold angels
Floating through the morgue with innocence
Eyes that want to live, then eternally close.

Bodies that fill up the room
You're embedded in there too,
Hopefully in harmony and serenity
I wish I could come and find you.
You're probably screaming for my time
But all I can hear is crying -
Whistles and light raindrops
'I miss you,' I really pine.
There's a bell inside my heart
Ringing with no intentions to stop,
Hopefully it will never run out
Like staring at a church, the cross withering on top.
I miss you, as I walk around in the morgue.

The faces, new and old
Nothing like the complexion, so fair,
Say a few words
For the beauty that lay there.
Pure souls - ever forgiven
Floating underneath the closed palms
Miming the sign of the cross.
Eyes that want to close then sink -
Well, maybe you would understand
If you had entered the morgue.

Michelle Proby (15)
Newcastle Bridges School, Newcastle upon Tyne

Bitter

Love's first bite
Its taste is intoxicating, no?
Its tender nibbles
Its lustful marking
Its animalistic claiming
Just whose are you, my sweet?

Sweet, sweet temptation, adorning red and purple
Colours of love and passion.
Of desire and lust.
Of roses and lavender.
Of blood and bruises.

I know how you're feeling from the simplest of touches
Needy - needing affection, familiarity
I'll be pliant - give you gentle hugs when need be.
I won't let on
Let you know the thoughts that race through my head.
Racing, racing hard and fast
Trying to keep up with my heart,
Slow and steady wins the race, sweetheart.

Until it all changes
And the game becomes feral, wild,
The animal inside me reacting to your heat.
You're so close.
And then sweet temptation will taste so . . .
Warm? Salty? Metallic?
Perhaps . . . probably.

Sweet temptation will taste so bitter.

Stephanie Gallon (16)
Newcastle College Sixth Form, Newcastle upon Tyne

Decrepitude Of the Mind

(In memory of Nan)

The sadness of madness
Reigns in others alone
Because the mad are always glad
Of the things they don't know.

The confused and bemused
May upset and grieve us greatly,
But there's no fear of shedding tears
When there's no knowing 'then' or 'lately'.

When you can't find your mind,
You don't search the living space,
You don't keep to words or ways,
Or remember every face.

Your world's instead inside your head,
Imagination rules -
And thus the sadness of madness:
Imagination makes us fools.

Laura McCahill (15)
Norton Hill School, Radstock

As I Walk Down The Lane

As I walk down the lane,
My heart feels glad to be back again -
To see the purple raindrops and to hear
The chatter of birds in the trees.

As I scuff my battered shoes on the damp ground,
I kick a bit of moss away,
Only to find more as I take another step.

As I look up at the sky I see a flock of starlings,
Small and spotted,
Flying gracefully over the full branches,
Up and away over the fields.

As I take a deep breath and smell the musty air
And odour of the blackberries and overgrown bushes,
I say to myself with an air of satisfaction,
'This is the beginning and the end . . .'

Minna Davies (11)
Norton Hill School, Radstock

Killer Nightmare

I ran, it was terrible,
It was like I was in an old video game.
You are at the end just facing a new level.
And it was harder and harder,
Death chasing me like metal to a magnet.
The forest was a terrible place to run.
The dead, claw-like trees
And the roots crawling like an infection on the floor
And then a tall tree swinging round it,
Now it's catching up.
Then . . . I wake up.
I am breathing heavily,
What a nightmare.

Matthew Barnett (12)
Norton Hill School, Radstock

Nightmares

It terrifies an adult,
It makes a child scream,
You would not want to have one,
They are more than just a bad dream.

It writes over your emotions,
It can de-programme you completely.
It can make you shiver, yet sweat,
It doesn't take you over discreetly.

Every happy thought that blossomed,
It kills so ruthlessly.
It is programmed to destroy,
To tell you truthfully.

I am more than a bad dream,
I am a nightmare.

Natalie Cross (11)
Norton Hill School, Radstock

My Eternal Love

Thy hair be as black as the snow's be white
Thy skin be as white as the raven's wing black
Thou art dark and cold and empty as night
Thy heart, 'twould break if it held one more crack

Thy temper, 'tis fierce, ardent and severe
More so than the strongest storm on the sea
Thou has never been seen to shed one tear
Instead thou lets out an unspoken plea

As the trees still grow and the wind doth blow
As the birds fly south and always come home
As the fire burns and the water flows
I'll love thee always, wherever thee roams

When I breathe no more, my heart doth not beat
I'll still smile with content in idyllic sleep.

Lauren Thompson (16)
Norton Hill School, Radstock

7o

Prehistoric Life

Prehistoric life, an area of mystery.
From the Archean to the Holocene,
From Dunkeostes to Leptictidium,
The millions of years gone by.
4.56 billion years to now.
Prehistoric life, an area of mystery.
From apes to us, how we evolved,
First apes then creatures more intelligent,
But still a look-alike.
Next the first member of the genus
Ardipithecus radimus to Astralopithecus afarensis,
The Homo habilis, the first of the genus homo,
To homo ergaster, to homo neanderthalensis
To us all in 7 million years.
Prehistoric life, an area of mystery.

Kieran Symes (12)
Norton Hill School, Radstock

Ode To Emotions

Escape . . . the knowing of pain
Exclude . . . the fear of war
Embrace . . . the joy of laughter
Inhale . . . the comfort of happiness

Silence . . . your inner demons
Seize . . . your loving companions
Seclude . . . your desire and want
Sell . . . your so-called 'needs'

You can't silence emotions, they grow in you . . .
You can solve them but never seclude . . .
Try to explain? Still not solved . . .
So, who cares?
It's a part of me now . . .
I will never be rid of these emotions . . .

Mary Appleton (11)
Norton Hill School, Radstock

71

Eyes

Eyes can be anything you want them to be,
The porthole to everything we beings see.

They fill with anger, hatred and pain,
They flutter like butterflies out in the rain.

Eyes are a trademark, brown, green or blue,
They squint with a smile, sincere and true.

Inside your pupil, reflecting light,
It shines, it shimmers, glistens bright.

They produce tears that roll down your cheek,
Eyes can communicate but cannot speak.

They give us the privilege of watching the sky,
As the fluffy white clouds roll slowly by.

They see your love when you first meet,
Watching people walk down the street.

They bring smiles upon friends' faces,
Eyes can admire wondrous places.

From the moment we are born and with our first glance,
Till the moment we stand to take our first dance,

Eyes capture memories and hold them forever,
Like a beautiful sunset, a true, natural treasure.

Clumped up with mascara or covered in solution,
But never have they changed throughout evolution.

Even the blind know the wonder of sight,
They dream of vision every night.

Hate of vision I do despise,
For the most wonderful thing is to have eyes.

Bethany Carlisle (13)
Oxclose Community School, Washington

72

My Body

There's certain things about my body I just don't understand . . .

Why are my ribs called ribs when they don't taste like BBQ?
Why are my nails called nails when they aren't made of metal?
Why is my tongue called my tongue when it isn't attached to my Nikes?
Why is the bone in my arm called a radius when that's a thing in a circle?
Why are my toes called my tows when they aren't strong enough to pull a car?
Why are my eyebrows called my browse when they can't look for anything?
Why do people call their legs pins or stems when they can't hold fabric together, and hello . . . do I look like a flower?
Why is their another bone in my arm called the humerous when it isn't even funny?
Why is my nose called my knows when it knows absolutely nothing?
Why are my legs called my legs when they aren't part of a table?
Why are my bottom-half legs called calves? Did you just call me a baby cow?

The list just goes on and on!
So next time you look in a mirror,
Try to consider that worrying about your waist
Is a waste of time!

Deon McCully (13)
Oxclose Community School, Washington

My Grandma

My grandma is very beautiful,
Her smile is like a rainbow-tinted spray,
A great influence in my life,
She's special in her own way,
Throughout each and every day.

Rebecca Manning (11)
Oxclose Community School, Washington

73

Our Home

I know you're young and don't understand
That the Earth is getting destroyed,
But if you put in a bit of effort,
Mother Nature won't get annoyed.

You see, this is all that we have,
The grass, the rock and the rubble,
And if we don't do things to save our home,
We'll soon be in big trouble.

It's not just us that are getting affected,
The animals are going, one by one.
Don't just sit there, we can help,
We just need to put in some action.

Bit by bit we save our world
And people will survive longer.
The Earth will stay our families' home,
Together we become stronger.

Let's help this world,
It's the only one we've got.
Let's reduce, reuse and recycle.
Come on, let's give it a shot.

Taylor Borsberry
Oxclose Community School, Washington

The Poem I Wrote At Home

My dad and I sat down to write a poem,
It was really hard, we couldn't get going.
We thought of things to write about,
But nothing came to mind, we could think of nowt.
We had a rest and played a game on the television,
But after a while we picked up our pen and got back to our mission.
So here's the poem I wrote at home,
My dad got sick so I did it on my own.

Rachael Roeves (11)
Oxclose Community School, Washington

74

My Baby Brother

B is for beautiful!
R is for rascal!
Y is for you'll love him!
N is for never naughty

R is for right cheeky!
O is for oh, baby!
B is for bouncy baby!
E is for everything's new
R is for Rod, his little dog
T is for trouble with a capital 'T'

J umpy but not grumpy!
A b, his big sis!
M eg, his horse!
E nry (Henry!)
S howman!

P eople to see, places to go!
R acing around!
I ndependent!
C urious and cute!
E veryone, bow down to Bryn!

Abagail Price (11)
Oxclose Community School, Washington

The Deadly Silenced Village

Sitting in my room under the velvet black sky
I saw a knight passing by.
His steel-plated armour shone so bright
In the glittering moonlight.
I wanted to scream,
I thought it was just a bad dream.

I heard him gallop along the path
Leading towards the cenotaph,
Under the sky so high above,
A damaged soul searching for love.
I saw the shadows pass my room,
I awaited him to seal my doom.

I peered over my windowsill,
But there was no movement, it was still.
I clambered back into my nice warm bed,
The next morning the village was silent, like it was dead.

Caitlin Gray (11)
Oxclose Community School, Washington

Ode To Music!

Music to me is the best by far
Especially strumming on my guitar
Even though I can't play
Music makes my day.
The more I hear
The more I cheer.

With a dream of being a star
It is so close but also far
Rock or pop
Or even hip hop
Anything I do
It's always you
Oh wonderful music.

Samantha Johnston (12)
Oxclose Community School, Washington

Trying to Forget You

On the ground in the middle of the road
I'm sitting thinking of you.
I miss you and I want you but that will never happen.
Every day I look for you but you're never there.
At lunch I pick your favourite things
Because it makes me think of you.
I try and forget you and pretend that you were never there.
The pain I'm feeling when you're not here is unbelievable.
When I think of you everything goes black.
Birds fly over my head then a sudden chill flies up my back.
I can't see, hear or think of anything apart from you.
Why did you leave me?
We were perfect together.
I miss you,
I miss you,
I miss you.

Hannah Ridley (11)
Oxclose Community School, Washington

Onyx

Her fur is soft like a velvet coat,
Sparkly things, her cup of tea,
Fleecy blanket, cuddling me,
Her eyes shimmer like a precious stone,
She doesn't like being left on her own,
She likes playtime with her toy mouse,
She enjoys exploring in our house,
Sitting on the window sill, watching the birds,
Her miaows sound just like words,
At 13 weeks old we love her dearly,
When I am sad she makes me cheery.

Lauren Nutting (11)
Oxclose Community School, Washington

Crossing The Road

If you want to look good every day,
Then always look for a safer way
To cross the road at day or night,
Because crossing at a bend just isn't right.
So go look for a nice open space,
Because crossing the road isn't a race.
So go on that new space, okay?
If you want to go away safe today.
So follow these rules that are simple, see:
Look right, left, right,
That's how easy it can be.

Sarah Mulheran (12)
Oxclose Community School, Washington

You

You are my comfort, you are my hope
You are the reason that I can cope
My eyes close and hands press together
Repeating, 'I'll love you forever'
And with a soft voice I talk to you
Hoping you'll forgive the sins I do
Then I lay in bed just to wait
For you to relieve all my hate
A lot of people think this is wrong
My life spent loving you for so long
My one wish is them feeling like me
When no one is around, there you'll be
Please can you show that they can confide
Through life we're not alone, you're our guide.

Catherine Malcolm (15)
Priory Community School, Weston-Super-Mare

78

Abortion - A Crime?

When does a baby's life begin?
Conception?
When its little heart begins to beat?
When it hears your every word?
When it can kick with tiny feet?

Imagine that little hand that fits so perfectly in your palm,
Is this baby still unwanted? Can you still cause it harm?

Imagine little blue eyes fixed upon your smile,
Reliant. Vulnerable.
Can you really be this vile?

To kill a human with lips that may never smile,
Eyes that may never see,
Hands that will never hold another,
A body that will never be cradled by its mother,

To halt this heartbeat so small, to stop it in its tracks,
To make it die and then turn black,

Your heart too will never beat with the same rhythm again,
It will always be half a note within half a beat,
The hole shall never mend,

Your arms will forever feel unfilled and unsatisfied in some way,
You'll feel five invisible fingers curl around your thumb
As they hang onto you for love,
And that just won't go away.

Feel soft curls as they brush along your cheek;
A taster of what could have been.
You look at other children, with smiles like their mothers';
A sight you could have seen.

Jodi Parslow (14)
Priory Community School, Weston-Super-Mare

79

The Haunted House

Our gang of boys and girls,
Scared by screeching owls,
Crept by the black, spike-topped gates
Kept together by a rusty chain and broken padlock.
Behind them could be seen
The ancient castle in the midnight-blue scene.

'Is it haunted or is it not?'
Who's brave enough to find out what?

Am I brave enough to enter in?
The hallway looked extremely dim.
I must put my fear aside
To cross the threshold in a stride.
Up above candles glide
Across the lofty ceiling wide.

The dusty, creaking, wooden floor
Harboured large spiders behind each door.

Sounds echoing within this floor
Made me think more and more
That the murmuring voices
Were ghostly spirit noises
Awaking from the dead,
Swirling round and round inside my head.

This haunted castle has frightened me,
Which eventually caused me to *flee!*

Charlotte Humphris (14)
Priory Community School, Weston-Super-Mare

8o

Back In Time

I lay down in bed
With a smile on my head
I went through the door
Wishing there was more

I had better get out too
If my history books are true
Although this was fun
Seeing a man run

I could tell he was adored
The crowd cheered and roared
Franz Ferdinand!
I recognised this land

With a whirr, a strange scream
Back into the time machine
I thought, it's time to go
I don't understand a thing, you know

It was the great R and J!
I realised I was at the play
Was I in the Land of Oz?
I wondered, wondered where I was.

With a whirr, a strange scream
This thing is a time machine?
I read the writing on the wall . . .
The monster looked from its height so tall

Covered in cloth, from its height it leered
Going downstairs, I saw something weird
This is going to be a great day
Waking up I thought, *hooray!*

Confused? Go back in time
Make the clocks re-chime
Start from the end
Confusion, it will mend!

Carrie Whitehead (14)
Ryton Comprehensive School, Ryton

81

The Pending Door

They tell us life is one big chore,
They're always so high strung,
But we just laugh, and worry not,
We can, because we're young.

There are no chains to hold us down,
No wrinkles in our brow,
Tomorrow is an age away,
When you only live for now.

So we throw our hands up to the sky,
Dismiss the pending door,
And we join in with the laughter,
Of the ones who came before.

Their words still cease to hinder us,
Their wisdom is but lies,
They speak through all their jealousy,
We see it in their eyes.

But the clock is ticking quickly now,
The years slide by so fast,
Enjoy this while you can, my friends,
For indeed, it will not last.

Amie Foster (14)
Ryton Comprehensive School, Ryton

My First Gala

I wait for the whistle to blow,
Energy getting high,
My coach shouting, 'Go!'
I know my stroke is butterfly,
My arms they flap,
I lash,
I dash,
Making such a mighty splash,
The finish line, metres away,
The roaring crowd saying, 'Howa, howa,'
I won, I won, I beat them all,
But it's not over yet, my next stroke is back crawl.

Bailey Kendal (11)
Ryton Comprehensive School, Ryton

Pollution In The Year 2050

It breathes smoke and fumes,
It poisons the water,
It covers the land
With rotten food and rubbish.

It captures the scenery
And locks it away,
It turns hope to despair
And laughter to tears.

It blinds the fish
As they push through filthy waters,
The rocks growl
And crumble to the ground.

All hearts stop beating,
All smiles turn to frowns,
The little girl cries,
Pollution wasn't so kind this time.

Anastasia Sewell (12)
St Gregory's RC School, Bath

Moon

Glistening white amid stars in the night,
Projecting its fluorescent, milky light,
Calm and beautiful in the midnight sky,
Millennia old, still watching time pass by.

In a permanent swing around star and sphere,
Looking down on Earth saying, 'Nothing out here!'
Shadowing us in a dance without end,
A mysterious wonder, yet our eternal friend.

The farthest man has ever been,
Tranquil sea, empty but so serene,
Filling the sky with a light so pure,
A being so old it can always endure.

This once molten orb of liquid rock,
Flung into space with no time to take stock,
A lonely ball, sister to Earth,
Partners in the heavens, since before our birth.

Joseph Croucher (13)
St Gregory's RC School, Bath

84

My Glorious Sweets!

In the corner of my eye I see
Something shimmering, hmm, some sweets.
I take one step and stretch my arm over to one.
Yes! It slips into my hands,
I then delicately unwrap it . . .

Open my mouth, inside it goes,
Fizzy and sweet, with the smell of a rose.

Delicious and tasty, truly yummy,
Scrumptious and bubbly in my tummy.

A most divine and succulent taste on my tongue,
Just like a dainty flower inside me had sprung.

Vibrant and dazzling colours whirl in my mind,
The radiant sights together all bind.

The bright, stunning colours make me dazed and dizzy,
Because of the taste: delectable and fizzy.

Zooming through my body an exquisite sensation,
To eat more sweets is my hugest temptation!

I grab two more meticulously wrapped sweets,
Or maybe three more, maybe four more, or . . .
The whole lot!

In my inviting mouth the luscious sweets fly in,
All the glistening wrappers ending up in the bin.

The heavenly flavour oozes down my throat,
An enchanting feeling, almost like I'm afloat.

I've devoured all the sweets that I truly adore,
But, between you and me, I really want more!

I search really hard, almost everywhere around,
But sadly they're finished and still not found.

Maybe I am a bit full?

I've given up and feel slightly uneasy,
I hug my tummy that feels quite queasy.

85

I miss my sweets but I am slightly full!
Surely it's not my sweets which make me feel so dull?

I'm full up from bottom to top,
But ooh, look, there's a lollipop . . .

Nadia Ghauri (11)
South Wilts Grammar School, Salisbury

Jump

I stand here,
All alone and scared,
Under the willow tree,
Staring down
All the way
To see what I can see.

I look down,
Paralysed with fear,
The water shimmering bright,
Gazing down,
Thinking about
What happened to me last night.

I cry tears
For the little girl
Whose dad comes into her room
And does things to her
That she does not like,
While all she's thinking is doom.

I inhale sharply,
Ready to go,
The rocks start to blend,
I'll count down from three.
I've jumped off the edge,
My life has come to an end.

Karina Walker (13)
South Wilts Grammar School, Salisbury

The Earthquake

A low rumbling sound
Comes from underneath the ground
Things fall and crash all around you
You try to find somewhere to run to

You manage to escape -
Just as the building collapses behind you

The earthquake that took so many lives away

You lie there, trembling
One last crash and then . . .
Silence
You feel like the only person alive

You stand up and stare at the broken city
Tears prick your eyes

The earthquake that destroyed the island of Haiti
The earthquake that took so many lives away

You feel the ground starting to shake
It is happening all over again

You do not know how long you have been trapped
When you wake, news reporters are all around you
You feel strong hands gripping you
Pulling you out of the rubble

The earthquake that tore families apart
The earthquake that destroyed the island of Haiti
The earthquake that took so many lives away

You see people being pulled out of the rubble - alive
You close your eyes and hope for another miracle.

Joanna Starling (12)
South Wilts Grammar School, Salisbury

87

Lies

There's nothing to fear but fear itself,
That's what they always say,
But if I was to give you advice,
I'd say fear is scary any day.
People use fear to show them what's real
In a world that's often fake.
So what are you scared of?
What do you run from, when the time is late?

I use fear to show myself that I'm still alive,
Like pain you can use it to help yourself survive.
If I cared, I'd tell you not to be scared,
But you've got to see the proof.
In a world like this where people lie,
You've got to see the truth, need the truth.

Have you ever felt pain so unbearable, felt it like me?
Have you fallen in love, true love, only to pay the fee?
Yes I know how you feel, I can relate to you, my dear,
Tell me the truth in a world of lies, just don't get too near.

Have you ever felt that you're the only one to truly see?
To see through lies to hear the cries but be unable to help?
You can see in my eyes, sacrifice, what did I give up?
It's on your lips, don't say it, don't drink from the poison cup.

Poppy Iveson (12)
South Wilts Grammar School, Salisbury

The Perfect World

When you think about it, everything has a name,
So much work and effort, stored up every day,
Yet we never stop to think and value our lives,
If we looked a bit closer and believed in ourselves,
Our world would be better.

People would have homes, food and love,
Animals would have hope because
They would be given a second chance,
The forests would live again and we
Would think of ways to help them,
Even tiny creatures we don't care for one bit
Could live their lives in peace, just left
Where they are happy, and everything would fit.

If we relieved our world from crime, war and anger,
Things would be better and peace would come out from under,
Isn't that what we want?
Isn't that what life is about?

Just stop and think,
Pass the message on,
The world is wonderful,
Please don't let it suffer.

Rosie Mabb (11)
South Wilts Grammar School, Salisbury

That Sinking Feeling

Deep blue ocean,
Shimmer, shine,
Ripple in the moonlight,
Shimmer, shine,
Sparkle in the twilight,
Shimmer, shine.

Plunge through the surface,
Glimmer, gleam,
Deeper, delve deeper,
Glimmer, gleam,
Freezing in the water,
Glimmer, gleam.

Ice all around me,
Dazzle, glow,
Darker and deeper,
Dazzle, glow,
Dark blue nothingness,
Dazzle, glow.

Resting on the seabed . . .
Sunken!

Natasha White (12)
South Wilts Grammar School, Salisbury

The Shadows

When the night falls,
The darkness calls,
Calling out to the people we love.

They slip away
'Til the break of day,
No matter what we say to stop them.

The shadows hide
The horrors kept inside,
Hidden in the human soul.

When they leave for the night
They think they'll be alright
If they stick with a group of friends.

But we all know
Safety's just for show,
But happiness always ends.

Ellen Emmins (12)
South Wilts Grammar School, Salisbury

Sonnet For A Teacher

For many years a special someone trains
To take up on that responsible role,
Educating young people's brains,
Schools need teachers to be their life and soul.

A teacher is such a special someone,
They have to be good and kind and fair;
A fine teacher can be what makes school fun,
But! With other teachers you don't compare!

For you are the very special someone
Who encourages the minds of the students
That you care for. You judge no one,
And your smiles and praises are well meant.

I am so glad that my teacher is you,
I wish that every teacher was just like you!

Katy Salter (17)
South Wilts Grammar School, Salisbury

Crazy

Some people think I'm crazy
But I just think I'm lazy.
I cry when I eat veggies
So I get called a baby.
I sometimes eat roast dinner
But not without my gravy.
When we go to the park
My sister picks a daisy.
The only person I find
Quite weird is the Maisy mouse.
I find my eyesight hazy.
Now you think this rap
Is my coolest zap,
But no, now I'm going to take my last nap.

Ahmed Motara (11)
The Crypt School, Gloucester

Warpig, Nothing But A Memory
(Inspired by 'Replay' by Iyaz)

Warpig, nothing but a memory,
In my head that I want to get rid of, but I can't,
Got me thinking like every day,
It's like this memory is stuck on replay, replay-ay-ay-ay,

Warpig, nothing but a memory,
In my head that I want to get rid of, but I can't,
Got me thinking like every day,
It's like this memory is stuck on replay, replay-ay-ay-ay,

I remember the first time we met,
He was at the mall with his friends,
But then he signed up,
He was hoping the army would give him a chance,

Who would have ever known
That he would make it in,
He never broke the rules,
He would march again and again.

He read something on a poster,
And that poster says,
'Join and get a gun in your holster,
You'll be running through drills all day.'

Warpig, nothing but a memory,
In my head that I want to get rid of, but I can't,
Got me thinking like every day,
It's like this memory is stuck on replay, replay-ay-ay-ay,

Warpig, nothing but a memory,
In my head that I want to get rid of, but I can't,
Got me thinking like every day,
It's like this memory is stuck on replay, replay-ay-ay-ay,

Battled all round the globe,
Not once did you die,
You'd battle on,
From night till the morn,

93

Doing things no one else would do,
You're like a chef but cooking grenades,
Battled all round the world,
But some day you are going to die.

He read something on a poster,
And that poster says,
'Join and get a gun in your holster,
You'll be running through drills all day.'

Warpig, nothing but a memory,
In my head that I want to get rid of, but I can't,
Got me thinking like every day,
It's like this memory is stuck on replay, replay-ay-ay-ay,

Warpig, nothing but a memory,
In my head that I want to get rid of, but I can't,
Got me thinking like every day,
It's like this memory is stuck on replay, replay-ay-ay-ay.

I could be your backup,
I'm going to stay by your side,
The one who helps you save some lives,
But I forgot to save yours,

Na, na, na, na, na, na, na, na, na, na, na, na,
Why didn't I save yours?
Na, na, na, na, na, na, na, na, na, na, na, na,

Now my ears are ringing,
Warpig, nothing but a memory,
In my head that I want to get rid of, but I can't,
Got me thinking like every day,
It's like this memory is stuck on replay, replay-ay-ay-ay,

Warpig, nothing but a memory,
In my head that I want to get rid of, but I can't,
Got me thinking like every day,
It's like this memory is stuck on replay, replay-ay-ay-ay.

Richard Baldwin (13)
The Crypt School, Gloucester

94

The Afghanistan War

When I joined up for the army four years ago,
My parents said it would be good for me and teach me a thing,
But oh, what they didn't know,
How everything in war just stings.

When I got sent to Afghanistan, I got really scared,
On the news I had seen all of the deaths,
And how those had truly dared
To breathe their very last breaths.

When we got there adrenaline took over,
I saw a lot of smoke
And thought I might need a four-leaf clover,
And thought how I might choke.

In the tank to the base,
I heard a great big boom,
I thought that I was going to lose my case
And end up in my tomb.

When we got out the tank we saw the damage done,
The bomb had caused a massive fire,
'Come on boys and grab your gun,'
Were the words of Commander Shire.

We ran over to the scene
And found at least 50 people dead,
I felt a pain inside my spleen
And a rush go through my head.

We knew there was nothing we could do
And went straight back to the tank,
And everyone's adrenaline grew,
But all our hearts sank.

When we got to camp,
We were greeted with lots of food.
Although the room was damp,
The ale was perfectly brewed.

The very next day we went out
To the Afghanistan border,
Here I had lots of doubt,
I was about to tell my mate but we were brought to order.

95

Two hours into the job
A bomb went off 200 feet from me,
I looked and saw nothing but heard a great big sob,
I then saw it was from my mate, Lee.

He had been hit by a large bit of debris,
That had come from a car door,
And then he shouted to me
That he'd love his parents for evermore.

It wasn't just Lee who had died,
But 20 or 30 men,
Who had tried and tried and tried,
And to those I say amen.

War is a horrible thing
That wipes out millions of lives,
It can be absolutely anything
And hurts like being stabbed with ten thousand knives.

Sam Haddock (12)
The Crypt School, Gloucester

Superheroes

They soar, unstoppable, powerful and brave,
Never to fail, never to stop,
As they fly past give them a wave,

Saviours for some, role models for me,
Keeping us safe,
Keeping us free,

They want no glory, just people to save,
We honour them greatly,
Never to lie in a grave,

We can always rely on our heroes,
Never let us down,
Always there to lift us up.

Brad Gregory (13)
The Crypt School, Gloucester

I Was Almost There!

I had been waiting for days,
Wearing my cramped boots and soggy clothes,
In the bottom of a carved hole,
A carved hole that stretched for miles,
A hole hosed down with wee and floating food extracts,
Like a sewer,
Where many men stood and many men had fallen,
To clamber over the edge,
The edge where your fate is never certain.

I looked around at the men littering the trench,
And to see the shadows of those whose bravery ended their life,
Their outline was shown with detail,
With either little movement or none at all,
I looked around, stopped and thought,
Maybe it was my turn to clamber over the edge,
The edge where your fate is never certain.

I clambered up the sloped, slushy, soaked sides
Of the protected trench,
Where my footing was never stable,
Because of the tread of our boots,
I ducked down low from the gunfire,
The sound of so many men's death,
My ears were ringing with the sound of screams,
Shouts far and near,
To clamber over the edge,
The edge where your fate is never certain.

I ducked and dropped to the ground, to the sound of a bomb,
It was as synchronised as dancing but not as meaningful,
I scrambled to my feet, turning up the mud,
But I still had no grip and my head was in full view of all guns,
To clamber over the edge,
The edge where your fate is never certain.

I then fell flat on my front, my belt dug into my empty stomach
And I began to think how hard it would be on a war field,
And I slid helplessly down, back into the trench,
Back into the pools of urine and mouldy bodies
Which the nurse didn't take away,

To clamber over the edge,
The edge where your fate is never certain.

I looked up at the edges of the trench that had defeated me,
But at least the war hadn't, or the bullet of a German.
I kept that in mind, but not to frighten me,
Or tell my grandchildren,
To show how strong and brave the men who made it up there were,
Even if the battlefield took them,
To clamber over the edge,
The edge where your fate is never certain.

I decided not to brave the trench sides,
Because the slushy embankment had already won,
Many other 'kids' tried it, but I would wait until the time was right,
In the winter where all the mud had frozen solid,
But I'm sure the cold or ice would beat me,
To clamber over the edge,
The edge where your fate is never certain.

Kieran Bird (12)
The Crypt School, Gloucester

The Princess Who Was Turned Into A Frog

Michelle is a princess who had a dream.
Her dream was to be a supermodel,
But she was a princess.
She went for a walk one day down the riverside,
Then at the tip of her eye there was a magnificent frog.
She started to gaze and gaze and gaze,
Then when she had him on her arm he spoke.
The princess was amazed and she didn't know what to do.
The frog was talking about when he was
Turned into a frog by the wicked witch.
He said he was once a handsome prince.
The princess looked into his eyes and then she kissed him.
Suddenly Michelle's clothes had dropped to the floor
And out came a frog.

Nathan Tout (11)
The Crypt School, Gloucester

Starlight

A beam of starlight, descending from a sky
Wearing stars as a shield,
Glittering and dancing along the crevices and cracks
Like a shower of diamond rain,
Clawing its way forwards, claws digging into
The shadows and tearing out their heart,
Gliding over the windows, swerving
In delicate intricacy of its unknown dance,
The dance of forgotten dreams and forgotten sorrows,
The dance of death.

The whisper of wings brushing the glass,
Their faded colours devoured by starlight,
The complex oval of a body with a conscious
Confined to a cage of dwindling life,
High in the tower searching for liberation,
Hunting freedom, the ever-escaping beast,
The beauty of a deity, the light touch of a mother,
Twisted into the screaming prisoner.

The bell sounds from below,
Its powerful call ringing through the tower,
The sound of worship and the sound of devotion
To a creature existing through myth,
The robed messengers walk below
As the silent guardians and unspoken captors,
The prisoner beats the glass in a constant rhythm,
The greatest of its blows worthless,
Her will starts to fade as the starlight grows,
Feasting on darkness as the night swells.

Her will broken and her body now in a casket,
She lies there, her wings fallen,
The starlight gazes upon her,
Its all-seeing eye penetrating deep into her very soul,
All it sees is longing, freedom and a dwindling life
Full of deep joy just out of reach,
As it gazes upon the prisoner it brings dawn,
Brings the light and the open window.

Matthew Brew (14)
The Crypt School, Gloucester

The Afghanistan War

I didn't want to leave my family to fight,
And no doubt I was about to face my plight,
Looking out of the plane window I was full of fright,
And when we touched down, I knew it was my time to fight.

On the Afghan ground,
The sun beat down like a burning furnace hitting the ground,
It showed no mercy for native skin or weaknesses
Of a foreigner within,
Beneath my every footprint, another crack seemed to appear,
Like a series of caverns waiting to draw me in to their lair.

Gunshots all around,
The skies ablaze,
Angry like a dragon's fearsome eyes,
My destination is Hell and I am slowly dying within.

Walking around I searched for enemy eyes,
Hoping and praying that I would stay in disguise,
But like dominoes, my friends fell,
One by one their screams and cries
Pierced through me like the sharpest of knives.

Waiting for my turn, I lay still,
Frozen to the ground as if encased in ice entombed in time,
The seconds, minutes and hours ticked by,
As my fears and questions went unanswered
In the deafening sky,
I slowly closed my eyes.

Not knowing when I would die,
I looked up into the dark night sky,
There a spark of light beamed down on me
And it was my time to shine,
Facing my fears, for I was alive,
I marched on a moonlit path into the night sky.

Max Harper-Emerson (12)
The Crypt School, Gloucester

100

War Poem

Young men were called to battle
To fight for country and king
Proud and brave, they carried arms
To fight a foe and try to win.

Those heroes didn't really know
What they were heading for
Or how many awful years
It would take to win the war.

So many souls tragically lost
To an enemy powerful and strong
Leaving folks back home to grieve and weep
Thinking how it's all so terribly wrong

Women and elderly could not fight
So they did whatever they could
Planting crops and keeping guard
Doing their best with rationed food.

The sirens would sound to warn them
Of the dangers above in the skies
As the bombs fell in their thousands
They ran to the shelters to hide.

Battles were fought all over Europe
But Britain would not give in
They could not allow the tyrant
To think he had a chance to win.

After six long years the fighting stopped
And peace was found, finally
But we still remember the brave ones
Who never made it back to Blighty.

Josh Izzett (12)
The Crypt School, Gloucester

The Battlefield

Something that is life
Describes as a whole
Keeps you up in the nights
And penetrates your soul

A battlefield
That all of us face
Get your armour and shield
But it can't be replaced

A lonely prisoner
Bound by the chains
Life becomes a blur
As it controls the game

You end up not in control
Of what you say and mean
But then comes your parole
And you become what you see

When they leave you
The clouds in the sky
Begin to weep
Using your eyes

A golden fortress
A place we all dream of
Something we all want
A time of being in love

So I thank you for the rights
From the bottom of my heart
For all the sleepless nights
And for tearing me apart.

Callum Webb (14)
The Crypt School, Gloucester

To War - Haikus

Trudging through the mud
All hope taken from us all
No looking back now

Climbing up the hill
We can hear the German troops
No looking back now

Guns are now firing
And soldiers are just dying
No looking back now

I shot a few down
But they get replaced quickly
No looking back now

I won't stop firing
But my ammo is too low
No looking back now

We are low on men
But the Germans are as well
No looking back now

Our leader cries out
'Retreat now, run for your lives'
No looking back now

I want the honour
I march to my death alone
No looking back now

It's my time to die
As a tear rolls down my cheek
No looking back now.

Matthew Fry (13)
The Crypt School, Gloucester

Intruder

Rush, dash, race and run, over flowers old and young.
Pan; tilt, up and down till the honey house is found.
The intruder will kill the grubs and adults true.
Lots of them are coming over;
They're not interested in our clover.
Our hive alive will be dead, the hornets feasting in our stead.
The queen must run before they hit,
Without her we will go bit by bit.

Rush, dash, race and run, over flowers old and young.
Send the chemical, call the guards,
Behind me they are just a yard.
All the workers grab the babies; of course there is only one lady.
Our time is short and running out,
Oh no, they're here, don't scream and shout.

Rush, dash, race and run, over flowers old and young.
I was too late, it's all my fault, quick get the door
And slam the bolt.
We must go out, delay them now, our stingers are no use so how?
To make them die will be so hard, our stories told to the bard.
Our lives all spent by twenty-three,
against our thousand and forty bees.

Rush, dash, race and run, over flowers old and young.
To mask the queen without her helpers,
to another place and shelter.
The slaughter is happening right this moment;
This shall be our one atonement.
Wait, what's this? The giants here, come without their nasty beer.
We won the battle for our cone; now let's go to our lovely home.

Harry Benbow (13)
The Crypt School, Gloucester

Poverty

Poverty, to which we turn a blind eye
Prolonging the cold, sorrowful cry
Of children and adults
Withering in the shadows,
This is not where they belong.

Poverty, opinions can vary
Whether deprived of water, feeling weary
Or starved of love, wandering the big city
Their only hope is to beg and beg
Until somebody finally gives them pity.

The question everybody asks is *why?*
The line still strongly lies
Dividing the rich from the poor
Even though our technology soars
Many are forced down to the floor.

Their knowledge of our world is dim
If they knew, their attitude would be grim
Our lives are full of greed, ever wanting more
But the truth is we are all to blame
If we look down deep to the core.

Our two lives can hardly compare
Even though we all breathe the same air
Their only hope is us, to change their ways
To resurrect them from the darkness
Using teamwork, we can pull them out
From the never-ending maze.

Alexander Cossins (13)
The Crypt School, Gloucester

The Life Of Warfare

As I wake up in dirty, wet trenches, gunfire starts.
I get up, grab my gun and take arms.
The warfare life isn't as I pictured,
It is much worse.

My troop and I charge into battle,
Shooting the enemy.
I call, 'Retreat to the trenches!'
We run back to the mud-filled trenches.

Then the enemy charges at us and fires.
All you hear is, 'Man down,' or 'I'm hit!'
It is a sorrowful sight.
Then silence.

I am alone with death all around me,
Then I hear a poor soldier shouting,
'Help me, please!'
I couldn't help him.

Then my friend, I saw him,
Dead on the floor.
Then darkness.
Am I dead?

Next thing I know,
My friend is dead
And I have lost one arm.
Why did I go to war?
I was too young.

James Bennion (12)
The Crypt School, Gloucester

Dreaming

I begin to drowse upon my bed,
I am beginning to fall to sleep
And my brain calms inside my head.

I begin to see but it's too misty and foggy to see.
It's like a cold winter night
But now I see! It's a pair of eyes looking at me.

They glow against the night.
It calls upon me and I stagger towards him.
I see his body covered in feathers and he bursts into flight.

What is it? I still don't know.
It's changing, it's losing its wings,
It's flying but it has no wings.

It's gone, but where?
No, now there's a beast,
It's tall and covered in hair.

No, now that's gone,
There's a lake,
A duck and a swan.

I see light, I am awake,
What was that place?
I think it was a dream, a mistake.

At least I'm back and glad to say,
But I'll be sleeping tomorrow as well,
I'll have to go back there. No, no way.

Benjamin Brown (11)
The Crypt School, Gloucester

The Trenches

Along the trenches we went,
The smell and sounds were horrific,
Showered with shrapnel and smoke
From the bombs landing around us.
'Duck and cover, lads,' our captain shouted
As a bomb landed in the trench in front of us.
The sound of fear and pain deafened our ears
As it echoed off the mud walls.

We waited by for the artillery to stop, that was our signal.
We climbed up the wooden ladder and
Charged towards the sound of the guns,
All hoping that we would survive.
Friends and fellow soldiers lay on the floor, motionless.
I carried on running, with the picture
Of my wife and family in my hand,
Knowing there was very little chance of me surviving.
We were just a distraction; the planes flew over our heads,
The sounds of our bombs hitting the enemy,
The sound of their screams,
It was their turn to be scared, not ours.

The posters back in England were wrong.
'War is just like a game of football'.
I wish I could go back to my family and friends.
I may have survived this time,
But tomorrow is another day in Hell.
This is just the beginning.

Joshua Bassett (12)
The Crypt School, Gloucester

1o8

Beast

Don't mess with the beast
You gotta realise that
I'll be getting the end pat
'Cause you're gonna be paying the fee
You're full of smiles now
Give it five and you'll be bowing
To the beast, so don't mess with me
Full of glee
Touch me and
I'll rub off that glee
Don't mess with me, the beast
'Cause you'll get battered
And be in shatters
Don't mess with the beast

Don't mess with me
You may have two feet on the ground
But when I've finished with you
You'll be underground
I'll be bounding
Travelling uptown
Then downtown
And I'll be spreading my sound
And you'll be pounding
So don't mess with the beast
'Cause I am the beast
Of all beasts.

Sam Evans (14)
The Crypt School, Gloucester

The Bleak, Dark Night

Blankets of mist smother the sky
Gunshots flicker and dance in the night,
Life is so precious
Brave men determined to fight.

Cries of help echo with despair
Scared bodies tremble with fright,
Mortar's crashing down like hail
Lives will be lost this night.

Shuffling shadows
As gun parts rattle,
Men stumble hopelessly
In this weary battle.

Gasping and choking
In this path of hate,
Blood-spattered friends
Await their fate.

The trenches steal memories
Ambition and hope,
I think of my family
I wonder if they will cope.

I feel at peace
As I walk towards the light,
Out of the darkness
Of the bleak, dark night.

Joseph Anderson (12)
The Crypt School, Gloucester

110

The War

I could hear the bombs in the background
Lighting up the sky
I could hear the bullets
I was sure I was going to die

I ran to cover
But nowhere was safe
Looking for a companion
They were all lying on the ground

I jumped to the ground
Thinking I'd be fine
I could hear the footsteps
I was living on borrowed time

The night sky surrounded me
The wind whistled through the air
I could feel the vibration of the bombs
I tried not to care

Engines screaming from enemy planes
Bombs being dropped from up high
I turned to my friend and said farewell
Almost sure I was going to die

I could smell the smoke
It choked me to the ground
Everything went silent
Then there was no more sound.

Tom Carter (14)
The Crypt School, Gloucester

Cars

Cars are all around us,
We use them instead of the bus,
Where would we be without one?
Oh, we would make such a fuss.

Some are slow and some are quick,
You can really take your pick,
But when they won't start,
You'll end up giving them a kick.

As you turn the key in the ignition,
You can hear the engine roar,
Stamp your foot down on the pedal,
You will leave tyre tracks on the floor.

There are so many different makes,
From an Audi to a Zonda,
There are so many different models,
From an R8 to a CRV Honda.

My favourite is the Maseratti,
It looks so sleek and cool,
You have to be rich to buy one,
It uses tons of fuel.

Cars are all around us,
We use them every day,
They get us to school and work,
And back at the end of the day.

Sudi Webber (12)
The Crypt School, Gloucester

112

The Unsung Soldier

He is known to the world as a soldier
Who stands at the gates of dawn.
He is known to his sergeant as Private Slacker
His soul went to the end of the Earth.
Like stars flying through the solar system
They run to greet their own,
With voice of flame they sound his name
Who died to us unknown.

He is hailed by his family,
By the Dauntless of Marathon,
By Raymond, Godfrey and Lion Heart
Whose dreams he carried on.
His name they call through Heaven
Unheard by Earthly ear,
He is claimed by the famed everywhere
Who knew no title here.

Oh faint was his battle cry
And dim was the Milky Way.
Oh far was the floor of paradise
From the soil where the soldier lay.
Oh chill and stark was the sleeping dark
Where huddled men lay deep;
His comrades all denied his call
Long had they lain in sleep.

Alex Williams (12)
The Crypt School, Gloucester

Food Chain Poem

There was a little worm crawling in the dirt,
Until a little bird came down and ate it,
However the little bird did not escape,
It got eaten by an eagle for its supper.
This was the end of all the eating
Because the eagle was at the top of the food chain.

Ritesh Patel (11)
The Crypt School, Gloucester

113

Torn Apart

It uprooted trees
Razing homes to the ground
It spread like a disease
Screams of children were all around
It aimed at anything in sight
And nothing could survive this dreadful might

People ran in and out with the tide
Nowhere to go and nowhere to hide
Sweeping hundreds off their feet
Loved ones being torn apart
People running up the street
As it found a way into everyone's heart

But no one knew what was on the way
People were at work
And children were at play
The sea gave a slight smirk
As the tide went in and out
And even further and further out

Lives were lost, bodies were found
Brutally killed by a hungry hound
Most people did not live to see another Christmas
The few that survived the Sri Lankan tsunami
Understood the meaning.

James Fleming (13)
The Crypt School, Gloucester

114

Life Is Like A Stream

Flying through the air
Past the birds and planes
Wait till it gets cold enough
And plummet back to Earth

Bob round the rocks
Explore hidden coves
Race down a waterfall
Splashing as you go

When you come to
The end of the stream
Down the estuary
You know it's the
End of the line
In the deep blue sea!

Round the coral reef
Following the current
But when it comes to evaporate
You'll be left alone

Life is like a stream
It has its ups and downs
Fishes come and go
But you just flow along.

Jack Gisby (11)
The Crypt School, Gloucester

The Spirit

He was once a man.
He once walked the same world as us.
But he is coming.

He was once an orb of respect.
He once held a sword.
He was once a hero.
But he is coming.

He is coming for revenge.
Revenge on the people that thwart him.

He was once a lord.
He was once a soldier.
He was once a king.
But he is coming.

He was once thought as a god.
He was once treated as a role model.
But he is coming.

He is coming for revenge.
Revenge for betrayal.
For he was betrayed by his friends.
Set up and killed.

And thus is the spirit Lord.

Benjamin Standen (12)
The Crypt School, Gloucester

New York

The traditional yellow taxis swept along the road,
Hailed from the street and paid what they're owed.
The lights of Broadway lit up the street,
As night duty workers sat down to eat.
The crowds of people bustled as they shopped,
Shopping all night, shopping 'til they dropped.

The tourists walked, unfazed by the night,
They went to the Empire State for a view of the light.
The Statue of Liberty, a beacon of peace,
For this is the city that never sleeps.
The Smithsonian Centre stood proud,
Macy's made money from the entire crowd.

The taxi engines groan from the work,
As the taxi driver went berserk.
In the natural history, lights dimmed on the coliseum,
For this was night at the museum.
Central Park was quiet tonight,
But Times Square was incredibly bright.

All the lights filling the city,
As no one is there to pity
The taxi driver, whose car has no torque,
But who cares? This is New York.

Matt Hartshorn (14)
The Crypt School, Gloucester

War's Authenticity

Their faces hung, the envelope on the floor,
Conscription was awful, it was happening more.
The old and the young, the rich and the poor,
All made to comply in this hostile war!

They thought it would last a month or a few,
What they really were doing, nobody knew.
Days and weeks passed, further casualties died,
Information we heard, all propaganda, they lied.

Fields of bodies, trenches brimmed with blood,
The rain - it poured, men dressed in sludge.
Trench foot, bloodied men were a common sight,
But still they fought on, with supplementary might.

The more they hoped, the more they cried,
Emotional hurt led to suicide.
They didn't expect this, so many lives lost,
Weaponry and bombs - this war undoubtedly cost.

Children unknowing where their fathers went,
They didn't really understand what war and fighting meant.
The tears and the upset, the families it tore,
How brave were these men;
Their country they risked their lives for.

Bradley Palmer (13)
The Crypt School, Gloucester

I Wish I Never Went

The mortar came down, I had to run,
I saw my friends fall from the bullets of a gun,
My feet were sore, I couldn't walk anymore,
The puddles turned red,
It was as though everyone was dead,
The trenches smelt,
There was such heavy gunfire I couldn't tighten my belt,
I knew I should have never went.

Luke Stephens (13)
The Crypt School, Gloucester

118

The Book

The book that wields thou mythical beast
Sings in the moonlight and dances in the light,
Never stopping, eternally mischievous,
Through the freezing, misty night it uncovers its verses.

The aging ancient book that wields thou mythical beast,
Its pages crumbling but never dying,
Forever knowing but never perishing.

The beast soared through the imaginary world in that book,
It screamed as loud as a rocket,
But was 'fraid as a wolf hunting viciously
In the half-lit sky,
However the beast was as useful as a baby
Cos it was trapped in the book. Trapped. Dead.

The book that wields thou mythical beast
Sings in the moonlight and dances in the light,
Never stopping, eternally mischievous,
Through the freezing, misty night it uncovers its verses.

The book that wields thou mythical best
Laughed at the humble, ignorant humans,
It was as silent as an angel but
When all was silent, the pages once again bristled to life.

Zakkaria Raja (12)
The Crypt School, Gloucester

119

The Trenches

The brave men defending their country,
In the cramped trenches.
Stray bullets whizzing overhead,
Friends dying around them.
The terrible food they were forced to eat,
To keep themselves alive.
Lying there at night,
Not knowing if they were going to live or die.
Sitting there in the mud, dead bodies all around them,
Not knowing if they were going to live or die.
Memories of friends and family in their heads,
Wondering if they'd ever see them again.
Sat there in the mud wondering, *why am I here*,
Will this ever end?

Their families sat at home,
Wondering if they were going to get bombed.
Worrying if their relations would die
Fighting in the trenches.
Fearing the enemy would break the barrier,
Wondering what would happen to them if it happened.
All their hearts lie with their relation in the trench,
Not knowing if they were dead or alive.

Sam Bell (11)
The Crypt School, Gloucester

120

The Fiery Dragon

The fiery dragon, tall and red,
If you're not careful he'll burn your head!
Fiery as the scorching sun,
Braver than the mighty phoenix,
If you don't give him the best of fun,
You'll get 80 kicks!
Wings with scales, all very thin,
If he enters any race, his wings will make him win!
He breathes fire with devastating force,
It's more magical than any wizard's sword.
Eyes as green and shiny as emeralds,
They have the sparkle of a star.
His teeth as sharp as icicles,
They can even cut through diamonds.
The tip of his tail reaches the River Severn,
His head goes up into Heaven.
He has the hearing of a bat,
He has the senses of a rat.
He flies at the speed of light,
It gives others a big fright.
Now the day is over, he enters his stone cave
To spend a peaceful night.

Bradley Mayo (11)
The Crypt School, Gloucester

The Platoon In Peril

Feeling tired and weak,
Trying to find the cover that we seek,
Bullets randomly flying,
People all around me dying.

Air support won't be here for some time,
Reinforcements are being primed,
The images keep repeating, they are all the same,
All of my squad's bodies lie still and lame.

My comrades have fallen, I'm on my own,
When suddenly I hear a pitiful moan.
As quick as I could, I ran to his aid,
When I saw him I knew his fate was here laid.

His severed limb,
Hanging on by a whim,
As the chopper arrives,
I know he will survive.

This, my friend, is a tale of
Nightmares and horror.
Never get caught by
The false truth of war.

James Cheveralls (13)
The Crypt School, Gloucester

Silent Night

As the owl flings itself
Across the night sky,
It is ever as shy as it flies.
You only hear
The beating of its wings.
As it lands as silently as ever,
You gasp at its grace.
This is the only time
You'll be fortunate enough to see this.

Hayden Burford (11)
The Crypt School, Gloucester

122

Hyperspace Galaxy

Silence and stars, suspended in time
The undiscovered galactic region
All is dark, no life, big or small
The blue planet of Earth alone

Comets crash down, whirling like a hurricane
Splitting into dust never to be seen again
Burning through the atmosphere, frying like an egg
Crumbling into nothingness

The red spot of Jupiter, the raging storm
The gas-ridden planet so far from the warm
The choking fumes suffocate
Never explored before, we'll have to wait

The lunar moon stuck in a cycle
Orbiting slowly round the Earth
Though it's not made of cheese
We explored it with ease

Satellites and supernovas across the universe
Other life may be out there
Though it's unknown about the end of the world
Make the most of the precious time.

Alex Lipscombe (13)
The Crypt School, Gloucester

What Is It?

There he was, lying on the floor
Dust collecting on and inside him
He slowly breathes, every breath is a challenge
Slowly the light from the open window illuminates his face
Hundreds of creases and cracks were on his pale face
Flies all over his head and shoulders
As if they were eating him away.
Then I am wondering . . .
What is this?

Alex Wasley (11)
The Crypt School, Gloucester

123

Change

Life stays the same
With routine checks on the hour.
If people go insane
They are stopped by men with power.

Life does not change,
When those who try are stopped.
When people acting strange
Are never left to carry on.

The world continues
With check-ups frequently.
When people blow a fuse,
They won't continue easily.

Without a difference to be found
People act happy.
When men are not being sound
They are blocked instantly.

When people start to argue,
Big cheeses intervene.
But majorities keep through and through,
They stop them being mean.

Liam Searle (13)
The Crypt School, Gloucester

124

During And After The War

Did you remember the 16th of December 1971?
The day Bangladesh saw their freedom and won
That day gave freedom for us
For we should get independence, we must.

Our brothers and sisters gave blood
To our ambitious nation,
Soldiers lay on the trench, lifeless
Buildings lay weakened or collapsed

But hope wasn't ended, we didn't give up
From help by our neighbours, we fought with unrest
The country strengthened day after day
Then one thing changed all this dismay,

The bases in Pakistan thought they had won
Then came India and Bangladesh forces, all as one
They launched a surprise massacre, killing 50,000
The commander and the other thousands

Employed themselves to surrender,
The day of 16th of December
Came to the world with the news of our independence for
Did you remember the 16th of December 1971?

Abeed Hassnat (12)
The Crypt School, Gloucester

The White Horizon

It's there, it's there, it's always there,
As far as the eye can see,
It never moves, it's never fair,
'Cause it's far away from me.

Sitting in my shelter,
Inside is only me,
I wait and wait and wait,
But it's all I can see.

I'm sitting in there all alone,
It's something I can't bear,
It's always in my mind
And it's the only thing worth there,

The sand is always scalding,
It simmers in the sun,
My skin is red and peeling,
And my whole body's numb.

My mind cannot contain it,
It will not pass the test,
Only the white horizon
Prevents eternal rest.

Jake Waghorn (14)
The Crypt School, Gloucester

Music

Music comes to life,
When life is boring,
When I am lost,
Music can cure me.

Sharing the feeling between all people,
Uniting all ages, styles and culture,
Breaking down barriers, a united language,
Music is my form of expression.

Singing in praise, gospel or rock and
A mutual expression leaving us hand in hand,
Awe and wonder, hopes and fears,
Ambition recorded through dreams of youth.

Music in my life creates a sense of control,
Helps me escape from pressure,
Something you can't take away,
It turns my night to day.

Music brings life from the ashes,
Bringing hope when all is gone,
Building bridges between weak and strong
Music can never be right or wrong.

Dylan Williams (13)
The Crypt School, Gloucester

127

The Beauty Of Bikes

The back wheel squeals,
The front wheel turns,
The hand is twisted
And the engine churns.
The air flows by,
Like a gull in the sky,
While others just stand and stare.
The speedo turns like a spinning top,
The rider concentrates,
But still the finish line waits.
Effortlessly it weaves through the traffic,
Gracefully it nears 100,
The engine is roaring
And the rain stops pouring.
The wind dances by,
Smiles fill the sky,
Everyone wonders why
This bike can't fly.
It's got 1,000cc,
But all people see
Is one of God's magical creations storming by.

Rhys Jones (13)
The Crypt School, Gloucester

This State Of Mind

When he is in this state of mind,
He's wishing he was blind,
Sometimes his life is confusing.

He feels the power of his grief,
He believes that death would be such a relief,
All the secrets that hide within him would die.

His depression is his only friend,
It drives him insane,
Why won't they let him carry on to a dreamer's sky?

I can hear him crying in his dreams,
Can you not hear his painful screams?
When he fades away, I will fade away . .
The fluid on his cheek,
It drains him, he becomes lifeless,
His heart is just cold and bleak,
Black blood, black tears.

To him his life is like a masquerade,
He is in debt to himself, but he just can't pay,
Eventually he will call it all a day.

Harry Moreman (13)
The Crypt School, Gloucester

The Phoenix

The phoenix flies around, flashing its many colours
As it silently glides in the night sky
It enters the derelict building
Finding nothing but a man close to death
The phoenix flies into the man's body
Penetrating a layer of skin
Flames shoot out of the man's body
Showing only a silhouette
The man walked out of the flames
With a phoenix perched on his back.

Harry Byron (12)
The Crypt School, Gloucester

129

Blood Is In The Air

The roar of the Kitty Hawks passed over the field,
Looking for a hint of life.
The squad looked as if it was cut by a long trench knife.
The sky was stained a grim grey, the rain a ghastly red,
The commanding soldier had been shot, straight through his head.

In the distance I heard the cries,
All the war posters were great lies.
The enemy Zeros circled them like flies,
The burning planes lit up the skies.

The enemy AA guns fired,
We frantically dodged until we tired.
My mates were fried,
The soldiers died.

I was shot down by the ace in number seven,
The last of my plane lies in Devon.
The eternal sun shines in Heaven,
I met with my son, only eleven.

What a waste of life.
I pray for my daughter and wife.

Matthew Smith (12)
The Crypt School, Gloucester

130

The Importance In People

It can light up the world and clear up the sky
It's the one thing that helps when saying goodbye
Just walk down the street thinking of good
Not anymore is this misunderstood
Wave to a friend and give someone a hand
Shout to the people that you now understand
Fight for the world, give it what it needs
Don't let the Earth suffer and bleed
Care for each, let the room shine
Look for answers and let fate intertwine

Keep what is valued; yes, keep it by your side
Remember everyone, everybody, worldwide
Your conscience is good, it guides you through
Look deep inside for what is subdued
Everything is not what it seems
And so that is why 'I have a dream'
Do what is right and do what you should
Look in your heart, see what is good
The importance in people is way overdue
Just smile, it's the best we can do.

Zak Mitchelmore (14)
The Crypt School, Gloucester

Death Dies

The dread of life, our immortal fear
Like a thumping hammer pounding the hourglass of life
The cracks start to show like a wall made of solid time
Crumbling in the time-ridden wind.

The wind's howl creating crevices of time
Life coming to an end
Each crack a time hole telling tales like an old woman
The woman's voice telling the tales of a thousand lives
Each story slowly killing a man
That man holds his heart, says his prayers and hopes.

Joshua Winkley (14)
The Crypt School, Gloucester

131

Shadows Of The Vampire

In Man's darkest hour, the petrifying monster awakens.
During times of great chaos, the world shall hear
The ear-piercing song of the vampire.

Searching for lost souls, he will leave his threatening mark,
An evil plague upon the world.
He will force the spirits of the dead to walk by his side,
And enter into the land of the living.

Burning down villages, reducing them to ash,
For those who draw breath, their time is done.
His pale, icy skin and menacing eyes
Shall chill the body to the core.

Silently he moves through the creepy night,
Swiftly as the seconds pass.
He shall dominate the gleam of the morning sun.

No one can resist the vampire's call,
His shadow will cloak the last glimpse of hope,
He will blanket the happiness of all life left,
And then the age of terror shall begin.

James Lippitt (11)
The Crypt School, Gloucester

132

Bang

Stones
Rocks
Leaves on trees
Sky
Bang
Ice cream in the sky
Orange juice crashing at chocolate bars
Massive chocolate bars
Bang
Sand dunes
Grassy banks
Rock pools
Bang
Salt underfoot
Chips sticking out of salt
Yummy
Tummy rumbling
Bang
My walk down to the sea.

Daniel Barker (11)
The Crypt School, Gloucester

The Screams Of Soldiers

As bullets whizz through the air
People are dying here and there
Men who are hit fall back screaming
Someone is always screaming, screaming, screaming
The lucky ones are killed first
They do not have to wait in a sludge pit to die
They do not have to have nightmares about screaming
And wake to find it was not a dream
Bombs are dropped on you as you drop down
You wonder, *what for*? and *how much more?*
Your friends die because of a lie
As you pull the trigger of a gun
You wonder whose family will mourn tonight
You've got to stay alive in there
For the pain is something you cannot bear
And as you go over the top
Into a hail of bullets
You can think you had a try
Before you inevitably die.

Ed Spendlove (13)
The Crypt School, Gloucester

134

My Father Thought, I Am Proud
(Inspired by 'My Father Thought It Bloody Queer' by Simon Armitage)

My father thought, *I am proud,*
The day I came home after entertaining a crowd,
Half a century, the opposition growled.
Few balls later, I was bowled,
He said to me never get bowled, so I've been told.

And even then his face just frowned,
My heart went grey like the winter clouds,
Few more, and a feeling I was wrapped in shrouds,
But I kept my chin high and tapped the ground
At 49, I looked around and realised the silent sound
50 up on the board, finally my secret power has been found.

Continuing my innings, look around,
I felt that after this I should be crowned,
I was bowled and father was obviously down,
Then he says I should be uncrowned,
Everything around me seemed to be drowned,
But I knew I should keep high until the next showdown.

Arjun Prakash (15)
The Crypt School, Gloucester

The Trenches

The trenches,
Dirty, filthy, scary,
Whilst in them you ask,
'Will I leave this trench alive?'

We're knee-deep in sewage,
The stench stings your nose,
Your eyes water
And you just want to die.

People are dying by the second,
I fear I may be the next,
The next to meet death face to face,
Face to face, with pain.

The trenches are small and ever so damp,
No one can move an inch,
Misery is amongst us all,
Why did I agree to the torture that is war?
Why?

Oliver Pellatt (12)
The Crypt School, Gloucester

Raising The Flag

In the trenches of death we lay
Fighting for our king and country
The only reason we played
In their deadly little game

I saw all my friends lying on the floor
Weak and sick from what they've seen
They looked very poor
And we have been fighting for days

We advanced up the battlefield
Not knowing what was next
We only saw the trenches which were our shields
It was as if getting killed was by a high chance

After nine death-filled days
Our huge army that had hundreds
More than half lay
We raised the flag with no other reward.

William Bourne (12)
The Crypt School, Gloucester

Can It Be Real?

In the midnight sky, as my eyes commence to fade
I rest my head and lay down, seeing a glimpse of light
In the corner of my eye
What? Who? How? Why? These were the questions
Whizzing around my mind
Rising up from the top of my bed
I looked out of my window and saw a shadow
Moving swiftly through the dimness of the midnight sky
The shadow crossed the face of the moon
It was shaped in the form of an animal - a horse
But had a horn, long, thin and pointed
Could this be a unicorn?
Or could this be a dream?

Matthew Antonio (11)
The Crypt School, Gloucester

137

Silence Of The Guns

We waited for many days,
It felt like a hundred years.
Huddled in our sorrowed ways,
We felt and saw the tears.

Men ran out in open fire,
Floundering and fragile.
All were starting to fall and tire,
As they made us go that extra mile.

Mum, back home, is so proud of her boy,
The screaming will surely drive us all mad.
Ours is a world devoid of all joy,
We're all cold, frightened, lonely and sad.

The guns keep on blasting, but I hear them no more,
My gaze is transfixed by a radiant light.
The sticky blood oozes, but my body's not sore,
I whisper to the guns a final goodnight.

Sam Peach (12)
The Crypt School, Gloucester

The Candle

It twinkled in the window,
No thought of wafting out,
You could see the glimmer a mile off.
It wavered as if to grow,
Just touching the windowpane,
Thriving, the candle shrank,
Would it recede, die out?
All but a spot of orange prevailed,
A splutter of breeze sailed through the open window,
Gone.
The wick lost all life and the colour drained away,
A small dribble of wax made its way to the pool beneath,
No more of this candle remained.

Sam Durham (12)
The Crypt School, Gloucester

Unobtainium

There is a thing, it's always there,
It crosses space and time.
Its fruit and nectar is ever present,
Sweeter than the finest wine.

It's present in talks of earthquakes,
Of how a hawk will beat its wings.
Of birds and bees and flowers on trees,
Of cabbages and kings.

Like a tank it may charge,
Or a dancer it may float.
We might see it as a rose,
Or a beautiful pea-green boat.

This beautiful, majestic thing,
We think is hard to find.
But it is always there, you see,
As love is in our mind.

Hamish MacKellar (14)
The Crypt School, Gloucester

Dreams

My eyes gradually begin to droop,
My head slowly begins to lower,
I am plummeting down into a world of dreams.
My mind is seeing without the aid of my eyes,
And it is listening without the aid of my ears.
I am overwhelmed by the mystic hallucinations,
And I am blindly guided by my imagination.
I am bound with an impregnable seal,
And I cannot be released.
I have been hypnotised by the bewildering trance,
My dreams are becoming more eccentric and mesmerising.
Deeper and deeper I am plunging
Into the unknown abyss.

Chris Allen (12)
The Crypt School, Gloucester

The Unknown

I see nothing in front of me,
I see nothing behind me,
I don't see a thing at all,
But all I know is that I'm in the unknown.

I don't like not seeing a thing at all,
But also I like not seeing a thing at all.
I don't see a thing at all,
But all I know is that I'm in the unknown.

Something just crept up my leg,
I'm not sure what it was.
I don't see a thing at all,
But all I know is that I'm in the unknown.

Aha, that's what it is,
It's a streak of light from my window.
I now see a thing in front of me
And all I know is that I'm in my bedroom.

Jack Mackay (12)
The Crypt School, Gloucester

It's Raining Cats And Dogs

On a gloomy, gloomy day
Round about the end of May
Something changed in the sky today
It was raining cats and dogs

Dogs were falling from the sky
And the cats were trying to fly
People didn't get their umbrellas up
So they got knocked out by a little pup

Howling dogs and screeching cats
Were scaring anyone in sight
They were afraid about something painful
Maybe a little bite!

Kieron Millard (11)
The Crypt School, Gloucester

140

The Trenches Of Hell

Walking through the slush-filled holes
The hells of life portrayed
We're like little moles
A sick little game played.

Whoever told us war was good
Fighting for our country and king?
Why tell us all the lies they could?
Everyone just has to sing.

The hell-hole of life
Is just amplified at wars
With guns and knives
Where lots of blood pours.

I have to put my hands to my heart
And clutch tight
Putting the dead bodies on a cart
And feeling everyone's might.

Ashleigh Carter (13)
The Crypt School, Gloucester

The Sound Of Guns

The sound of guns, louder than they have ever been
I am about to go out and face my fear
I just looked out of the trench, it is the worst I have ever seen
The sound of the guns is the only sound I hear

Alright, this is it, I'm out
The bullets fly past my head
All I hear is other men shouting
I really wish I was at home in my bed

OK, I'm firing back
At the German men that shoot so well
Argh! A bullet! I am on the floor feeling slack
I'll see you in Hell.

Alex Smith (12)
The Crypt School, Gloucester

141

Into The Firelight

The heat from the flame, warming the darkness,
It warms up your soul,
Hot at the tip, just like an iron,
The impact is like a whip, burning the skin.

The light from the flame dancing in the darkness,
It lights up your eyes,
Yellow at the tip, just like sunshine,
The light is like a lamp shining over you.

The smell from the flame, lingering in the darkness,
It drifts towards your nose,
Tingling at the tip, your nose recognises the smell,
The smell is like a scent that you have smelt before.

The sound of the flame, breaking the silence,
Embers are crackling,
Crackling at the tip, just like fireworks,
The sound is like a clock, ticking every now and again.

Callum Hall (14)
The Crypt School, Gloucester

The Trenches

Walking through the trenches
With our hats on our heads
Sitting on our benches
Many are dead.

Walking up and down
Water up to our knees
It is definitely brown
Dead rats not eating our cheese.

Watching people die
Hoping to get home
Hoping not to die
Hoping not to break a bone.

Oliver Greensweig (13)
The Crypt School, Gloucester

When The Guns Stopped

Bullets were flying past everywhere,
People scrambling around for cover,
The sound of the machine guns filled the air,
Waiting for this war to be over.

There were dead bodies around every corner,
No sign of the end of this war,
The bullets kept coming
And that was what everyone saw.

Planes flew through the skies above,
Tanks patrolled the ground below,
Cars weaved through the bullets,
People limped away into the dim glow.

But people never expected this,
Everyone was shocked,
Nobody knew what was happening,
When the guns stopped.

Gareth Jones (12)
The Crypt School, Gloucester

Angels

The heavens open above me,
It releases rays of sunshine, hitting the ground,
A large figure slowly falls to the ground,
Its wings wide open,
The feathers reflecting the sun,
The white, delicate body, the pale face,
Its hand reaches out towards me,
Its gentle fingers shine,
I reach out and grab its hand,
A flash around us occurred,
I felt my heart pounding, I felt my body rise,
Swiftly we rose together
Towards blinding light,
I closed my eyes, I could feel its breath,
I opened my eyes, its face bright in the light,
A green flash burned my eyes, and it was all over,
I was back in the forest.

Adam Thurgood (11)
The Crypt School, Gloucester

My Father Thought

My father looked at me with pity and shame
Looked me in the eyes, dirty, I couldn't blame
Lecturing me on how I'm taking life as a joke
If I don't sort it out I'ma be like them crackheads selling coke

And even though I knew he was telling the truth
15 years back from being a youth
And I stand up with my mind stuck up with fear
Standing in shame with a droplet of tear

Looking forward 10 years from now, will I be in the good
Or in the same situation with my father who I misunderstood?
Time to change and see what fate lies ahead for me
Hoping that I'm wrong, my father is right and his wisdom will
have set me free.

Umar Heckbarally (15)
The Crypt School, Gloucester

144

My Father Thought . . .
(Inspired by 'My Father Thought It Bloody Queer' by Simon Armitage)

My father thought it was appalling
When I arrived home, the headmaster he was calling,
Broken in two, my jacket has a tear,
Made to look like a bear,
'Why couldn't you keep better care?'

Even now I though there were no issues,
Stabbed in the heart, my son's clothes broken,
Next time keep it tight or something might bite,
To attempt to break, yell and run for the lake,
The jacket soon disappeared into thin air . . .
Wonder why? Out came a glare.

The next day, the sound of tears,
My son's voice breaking as it nears
My jacket has got a rip. 'Well take it to the tip.'
And leave it there, until winter falls again.

Robert Murray (16)
The Crypt School, Gloucester

Nuclear Future

As I sat before the lake,
I knew the world would end some day.
Maybe today, maybe tomorrow, it was inevitable
That this world would be engulfed in sorrow.
I looked at my reflection in the calm water,
Realising my insignificance and how unimportant I am.
The calm water represented the peaceful Earth,
The Earth without us, monstrous creators.
Bombs, guns and death, that is all we have brought to the world,
And soon it will end us as quickly as we began.
Across the lake the Earth shuddered in fear,
A blinding flash of light, but I didn't blink.
My last thoughts as I sat before the lake were,
This world would end today.

Sam King (14)
The Crypt School, Gloucester

My Father Thought I Be A Fool
(Inspired by 'My Father Thought It Bloody Queer' by Simon Armitage)

My father thought I be a fool,
The day I told him the team for me be Liverpool,
As a Red he rattled his head.
Why not United instead?
'It makes no sense,' he said.

And even then I knew our teams were rivals.
Manchester and Liverpool, two of football's greats,
My father the one, I the subsequent of the two,
Both from the north-west, just 30 miles apart.
Yet I wear my colours with no fuss,
Our teams' rivalry never coming between us.

Now fifteen, I look back and begin to see
My team didn't matter, though it seemed strange,
A boy and his father's relationship is stronger than that.
Our bond, better than ever, that's the important stat.

Joshua Thornton (15)
The Crypt School, Gloucester

The Griffin

The griffin,
With its elegant wings,
As it flies through the sky
It blocks out the sun,
As it's very high.

With its divine power,
It rules the world as
The king of birds,
Every hour.

It flies through the sky
For all to see,
The king of birds,
Believed to be.

Spencer Curtis (12)
The Crypt School, Gloucester

146

The Best Ever Standard

My father's face was a state of beep,
The day Liverpool came back to sweet,
His jaw dropped, I belted, 'Alonso, you're sublime.'
This was only at the 3-3 point in time,
Considering the first half Liverpool were on a rapid climb.

And even if this was not enough, more was still to come,
Passes were dismal, with players' exhaustion at a max,
Some even with cramp and the drama had yet begun,
Tension mounted as penalties started,
Rival fans were in hysterics as Pirlo missed,
Milan supporters were asking, 'Is he p****d?'

Smicer stepped up confidently to score,
Shevchenko couldn't get it past Dudek, 'the closed door',
From beneath the cushion my face emerged with glee,
My father's face was a state of beep.

Matthew Couston (15)
The Crypt School, Gloucester

Blue Day

My friends, the blue day is here
The red ribbon covering the halls
The rooms filled with the laughter of children
Bright yellow cakes and bright green drinks covered the table

The people I knew sitting around laughing and smiling
Talking about how this day is great
Maybe they were right, or maybe they were wrong
The bell rings and we say our goodbyes

It was like moving up in the world
That must have been what they thought of it
The only thing I thought was
The sound of shattering bond deep in my ear
This, my friends, was the blue day.

Matthew Philps (15)
The Crypt School, Gloucester

147

Welcome To London

The weather is so grim
this house is so grim
and my body slips into
                    Polaroid picture . . .
your eyes are so grim
your talking is so grim
an electric fan and candle . . .
                    revealing our secrets
and a disconnected eye
make of pixie dust and a £5 note
not too thick but open enough
                    to inhale, to breathe, to die
now I am happy
alone . . .
          talking to the fog.

Pedro Mosquera (17)
United World College of The Atlantic, Cardiff

148

Stop, Just Stop

Constant voices hum
An everlasting murmur
Imprisoned in me

Stop, just stop

Screams dull to whispers
Yet my head is not my friend
Drive the voices out

Stop, just stop

Stainless steel saviour
The blade caresses my skin
Bleed the voices out

Stop, just stop

Red tears dance freely
Waltz on alabaster skin
Blood on the dance floor

Stop, just stop

Tears fall thick and fast
Relief, with the voices, bleed
Stain of existence

Stop, just stop

Empty silence burns
Soiled is the blade that bled clear
Bled away the pain

Stop, just stop

Now dry my red tears
Stop the dance of life and death
Live another day

Live, just live.

Jade Love (17)
Whitehill Secondary School, Glasgow

149

Onomatopoeia

I like noise
Rattling toys
Kids at lunch
And baby screaming boys
Kids at the bus stop playing a game
Ladies in their shop windows screeching
'I wish you kids were tamed!'
Old grannies weeping, 'My walking stick's broke,'
While grandad swallows the car keys
And begins to choke
This all sounds like madness
And doesn't sound cool
Probably at this moment you think I'm a fool
The crash
The wallop
Of doors at school
But you know what . . . ?
I love noise!

Harrison Millward (11)
Whitstone School, Shepton Mallet

How It Feels To Be Old

Age is not on my side.
And through tired eyes
I can see the world fading around me.
My ears are starting to stop working
And my legs feel like weak, wooden stalks.
I've started to watch television soaps
Like 'Coronation Street' and 'Emmerdale'.
My grandchildren come round every other week
And I sent them home full with sweets and chocolate.
I fear soon my time will be over
And I feel happy with everything I have done.

Ben Carroll (12)
Whitstone School, Shepton Mallet

How Does It Feel To Be Old?

How I would like to feel how it is to be old
Is it happy or is it cold?
Sitting next to the fire in a rocking chair
Looking in the mirror you see you have no hair
Drinking gallons of cups of tea
You suddenly realise you need a wee
Driving 1 mile per hour on the road
People saying, 'I can drive faster than you
When I'm old'
Your friends come round for Christmas tea
They see your three-inch Christmas tree
Your hands and face all wrinkly
Phew, I'm glad I'm still young and not that wrinkly.

Harry Burr (12)
Whitstone School, Shepton Mallet

Trees And Leaves

Leaves, leaves, they come from the trees,
They fall on the ground and go very brown.

Trees, trees, they have lots of leaves,
They are so brown and
They fall down.

Trees, trees, you can make
Lots of swings, the birds live in them
So don't disturb them.

George Hughes (12)
Whitstone School, Shepton Mallet

Mums

Mums always talk too much
Mums are as messy as such
Mums are as nice as bouncy beds
Mums think a lot with their heads
Mums, mums, mums, mums, mums are as nice
As you want them to be.

Jodie Perry (11)
Whitstone School, Shepton Mallet

Nan's House

When I arrived
In 1997,
She was always by my side,
I bet then she was my everything,
As she also is now.

She's my favourite family member,
I've loved her forever,
As far as I can remember,
She's always been there for me.

Her house is very cosy
And also quite bright,
The love and laughter
Make it feel just right.

The sound of the food sizzling
And the timer going ding,
The scent of homemade brownies
Makes me want to sing.

So this is here to show
It is my very favourite place,
And when I go there,
I feel real ace.

Latitia Williams (12)
Ysgol Gyfun Gwynllyw, Pontypool

152

Ode To Autumn

Oh Autumn, thou art beautiful
Bring squirrels to our autumn trees
And red berries as red as a drop of blood.
Give us the feel of the breeze
That blows the cold through our noses.
Let us see the night darkening
As black as a magician's cape.

When you come, the leaves start to fall,
The animals gather their food,
Preparing for the cold months that lie ahead.
The days start shortening as you enter our year.
The long days of summer feel far, far away.

Bring us excitement,
The thundering fireworks,
The bright colours of the Catherine wheels,
The rockets flying and zooming through the air,
The sparklers hissing.
Sitting by the bonfire, staring at the stars
As they sparkle and shine in the black night.
Oh Autumn, thou art beautiful.

Beth Jones (12)
Ysgol Gyfun Gwynllyw, Pontypool

153

Trouble In School

The bell's gone so kids can play
Teachers shouting, 'Do what I say!'
'You've been naughty so stay inside,
The way you behaved, I'm mortified!'
There's muddy fields so kids can fall
They're also fighting and having a brawl
'You're a naughty child, you always want attention
Yes, again you're staying in detention.'
There's wet grass and grey skies
There's rubbish on the floor attracting flies
'I hate school, it's not fair,'
Doing the class work is a nightmare
Walking through the hall where kids are singing
I'm very hungry but the dinners are minging
'Stop messing around, you're not a clown,'
'Keep it up and you'll be moving down!'
Everyone knows doing work isn't cool
But at the end of the day
We've got to go to school.

Jake Phillips (12)
Ysgol Gyfun Gwynllyw, Pontypool

ASDA Supermarket

ASDA, ASDA, the speaker announced
His voice excited as he eagerly announced
The offers in store were really enticing
The deal of the day was fruit juice and icing.

The aisles so enchanting, the lights and the sounds
The clanging and dinging and jingling aloud
They swayed back and forth the draught from the doors
With green and white labels they hang above the halls.

Children alike were pointing and calling
Their favourite goodies were eagerly calling
Mums and dads, full steam ahead
Focusing on the task ahead.

With hands like lightning, they scan the goods
Trolleys so high, invisibly pushed
The bleep and the ding, the numbers at the till
The looks on their faces as they pay their bill.

Ella Lewis (13)
Ysgol Gyfun Gwynllyw, Pontypool

Autumn

Yellow flashing leaves
Falling from the trees.
Little animals hibernate,
Ready for their sleep.

Everywhere you go
There are fireworks popping
And some other people
Are cutting the pumpkin.

Over in the corner
There's a bonfire starting,
Lighting up the sky
Whilst crackling and spitting.

Hannah Rosser (11)
Ysgol Gyfun Gwynllyw, Pontypool

155

The Trip To Disneyland

The excitement in my belly as I walk through the gates
I feel butterflies dancing and prancing on dates
I feel nothing more than happiness inside
That then shoots to my cheeks
And makes me shine a smile

The strength of the wind is really harsh
Which makes me very parched
As I queue for the rides I smell nothing
But candy and sweets
Which call to the children like their own weekend treats.

The speed of the rides
Is like nothing that you can ever think of.
As the night is drawing in
It's time for a picture with Mickey
And make my way home.

Jo-Hannah Davies (13)
Ysgol Gyfun Gwynllyw, Pontypool

War

War is a dark place,
A river of blood,
A city of death
And a world of hate.

War is guns reloading,
Death and blood,
Tears and depression,
War is a terrible thing.

At the start of World War I,
Soldiers went on foot or horseback.
Since then, military machines are better,
But war is still dangerous for a soldier,
They put their lives at risk.

Dafydd Rees (12)
Ysgol Gyfun Y Cymer, Rhondda

156

War

What is war?

In the time of the Greeks
It was old men fighting
And young men dying.

What is war?

In the time of the Celts
It was a fight for honour
Or for revenge.

What is war?

In the time of the Incas
It was a bloodbath,
Full of killing and dying.

What is war?

In our time
It is nothing like it was,
Some might say it is all of these.

Now the old and young
Die together,
It is more of a bloodbath
Than ever before.
Now it is a fight for survival.

Now it is a war
Of greed and power.

Ruth Davies (13)
Ysgol Gyfun Y Cymer, Rhondda

War

I'm flying high above a scene
Of destruction far below,
The dusty land that I just bombed
Is suddenly all aglow.

Time to fly home,
I've done my job,
I look below and
See the mothers sob.

Suddenly my radar beeps,
I hear a roaring sound,
A fighter jet, zooming past,
It spots me and turns around.

I'm face to face with my enemy,
It's a man I've never met,
I know whatever happens here and now,
One of us will not forget.

My target's on and so is his,
My finger's on the trigger,
Another plane comes into sight
But this one's much, much bigger.

I swoop, I swerve, I climb, I dive,
I fire all the time.
My plane is hit, my engines burn,
I've paid for my deathly crime . . .

Dylan-Siôn Hampton (13)
Ysgol Gyfun Y Cymer, Rhondda

Love

When I saw his bright blue eyes looking up at me,
I felt love.
When I helped him take his first shaky steps,
I felt love.
When I heard him mumble his first words,
I felt love.
When I watched him score his first goal,
I felt love.

When I saw him play Joseph in his school play,
I felt love.
When I saw his winning smile at the game,
I felt love.
When he passed his GCSEs with flying colours,
I felt love.
When I heard he'd passed his driving test,
I felt love.

When he dressed in his wedding suit for the big day,
I felt love.
When I saw my first grandchild,
I felt love.
The love you feel for your child
Is the greatest love of all.

Daniel Davies (13)
Ysgol Gyfun Y Cymer, Rhondda

War

War for love,
War for religion,
War for hate,
Open up Heaven's gate.

War for land,
War for greed,
More and more people bleed and bleed.

War for Man,
War for a world,
War for power,
It's all over the world.

War over money,
War over honey,
It's all the same,
Doesn't anyone find all this fighting lame?

War causes death,
War causes destruction.

People say men fight like animals,
But animals never had a war.
Now who are the animals?

Callum McLean (12)
Ysgol Gyfun Y Cymer, Rhondda

Love

Love is for that special someone
Right inside your heart
When that person comes along
His heart slots in that part

Then the feelings come along
That you've never felt before
You love the emotions you are feeling
And now you want even more

Those days you'll spend together
Are the days you'll most enjoy
You will even be together
When the both of you are annoyed

Everyone close to you
Will be around you one day
For you two to get married
On a lovely summer's day

When you are deeply in love
You want it to stay that way
But sometimes it's not meant to be
And the love just drifts away.

Taylor Hill (12)
Ysgol Gyfun Y Cymer, Rhondda

Love

Love is like a flower,
A flower opens up like the start of love.
At first the colours are bright,
It sounds amazing,
The crackling of the bud opening,
It's like the feeling of happiness,
The smell is so powerful,
It's fresh and free.
At first the flower is beautiful,
After a while it starts to lose its colour.
The smell disappears,
The beauty has gone,
The happiness sinks
And in the end, the flower dies.
Love will die also.
It becomes faded,
But there is always another,
A flower that grows from a seed.
Love will also grow again
And it will start all over again.

Elisha Rendell (12)
Ysgol Gyfun Y Cymer, Rhondda

War

Why? is the question we all ask.
Why are men and women out in Hellmand Province
Risking their lives for us?
They can't stop now because the Taliban are coming.
The bombs still popping, bodies still flying.

The attacks are still coming, the planes still flying
With dead bodies going through Wootton Bassett.
Why are they there?
Because of Tony Blair helping America.
When will it stop? No one knows.

Tomos Edwards (12)
Ysgol Gyfun Y Cymer, Rhondda

162

Love!

Love is simple
Love is true
I shut my eyes
And think of you.

Love is expressed
In many ways
Love is used throughout
Years, months and days.

Love is rainbows
Clouds and hearts
Love is a dazzling
Work of art

Love combines
The two of us
Fitting together
Like a leather glove.

But when all is said and done,
All you need is love.

Cerian Dunn (12)
Ysgol Gyfun Y Cymer, Rhondda

War Time

War and battles, fights and brawls,
Allies and Axes, guns and bombs,
Run, run, bang, bang.
1939, the air sirens roar,
1946, the torment no more.
There is no such thing as heroes in war,
There are ones braver for five minutes more,
But if you fight forever, you will die in war.
That's a reminder, what are we fighting for?
Whatever the cause, just remember
That death is just through the door.

Benjamin Owen (12)
Ysgol Gyfun Y Cymer, Rhondda

Love

Love is something that's hard to find.
Love can be right in front of you
But you still can't see it.
Love is something that can make you blind.

There is a soulmate for everyone,
Is what people say.
Where? And when? And how?
There is no way of telling.

Love is something you find
When you least expect it.
Love is something you find
When you aren't even looking for it.

When someone is happy when you're happy,
Sad when you're sad,
And looks after you when you're feeling down,
That's true love.

Stephanie Pearce (12)
Ysgol Gyfun Y Cymer, Rhondda

Love

Love is like a rose in the garden,
It is beautiful but you can get hurt easily.
Love is an emotion you cannot explain,
It's that gut feeling you have
When you know they're the one.
Love is something priceless
That you cannot buy from any shop.
Love is something older than time,
It is something that anyone or anything can do.
Love is like magic, you never know
How it happened, but all the same it's wonderful.
And when you've found love,
You will never be the same again.

Eilish Nicholas (12)
Ysgol Gyfun Y Cymer, Rhondda

164

Love

You have to be passionate for love,
Love can lead you to tears,
You have to be aware of these things.

Love can sometimes be hurtful,
It can also lead you to good things,
Life,
Dreams,
So here we go . . .

Love is blind,
Love is true,
No one knows
My love for you.
My love for my Emma,
She may be a horse, but
So pure!
That's love for sure!

Amy Jenkins (13)
Ysgol Gyfun Y Cymer, Rhondda

A Picture Of You

Pitch dark, nothing but bullets,
Flying in every direction.
Cramped and scared, shaking with fear,
Commitment and hard work,
Training for this day.

All to be heard, screaming and groaning,
Orders flying, bullets whistling.
Hard to keep moving, raw skin rubbing,
Wish it would end, can't keep going.

Close to my heart stuck in my head,
A picture of you keeps me alive.
Out of the darkness, a ray of light,
I look at you and keep on going.

Lewis Morgan (12)
Ysgol Gyfun Y Cymer, Rhondda

165

War

As the brave soldier
Stumbles to the ground,
He wonders how
He got here now.

Still marching with courage,
Avoiding the bombs,
Wondering what will go on.
Is peace around the corner?

They are in despair
While looking above
With the planes in the air.

He fought for his country,
He gave all he had,
Now he's lying on the grass
With death at hand.

Carys-Anne Richards (12)
Ysgol Gyfun Y Cymer, Rhondda

War!

War can be brutal
And fought in vain,
It causes many losses,
Leaves families in pain.

Side by side each soldier
Fights to escape death.
They defend each other bravely,
Some to their last breath.

Tour of duty over
And home they go,
Only the lucky ones,
But are they, though?

Chelsie Humphreys (13)
Ysgol Gyfun Y Cymer, Rhondda

166

Love

Be with the one that makes you happy,
The one that makes you smile,
The one that makes you laugh
And makes each day worthwhile.
Live for the moment,
Try hard to make it last,
Because life is so short,
It goes by so fast.
So when you find love
Don't let it slip away,
Hold on to it forever
And cherish it each day.
As long as you're happy,
Then it's what you should do,
Love that someone and let them know,
Before your life is through.

Holly Evans (13)
Ysgol Gyfun Y Cymer, Rhondda

Love

I love the way you look at me,
Your eyes so bright and blue.
I love the way that you kiss me,
Your lips so soft and smooth.

I love the way you make me so happy,
And the ways that show you care,
I love the way you say, 'I love you!'
And that you're always there.

I love the way that you touch me,
Sending chills down my spine,
I love that you're always with me
And I'm glad that you're mine.

Ebony-Marie Bourne (12)
Ysgol Gyfun Y Cymer, Rhondda

167

War

Running, shouting, firing guns,
Scared and upset,
Bombing, killing, shouting, throwing,
It's not fair.

I walk to find safety,
No safety is to be found,
I've lost my mother and father at war,
I am all alone in the dark.

I wonder if I'll live through this catastrophe,
I wonder if I'll live,
I wonder if my mother and father are alive,
Who knows? You never know.

Rebecca Owen (13)
Ysgol Gyfun Y Cymer, Rhondda

Love

Love is the best thing that could happen,
Love is many emotions,
Love can be stressful, happy, confusing,
Love is the way to express your feelings.

Love can make you feel warm and cosy,
Love can make you feel cheerful and happy.

It's easy to know when you're in love,
You feel all shy and wobbly-kneed when you're in love.
You feel like you have butterflies in your stomach
When you're in love.

Trust me, it's a wonderful feeling.

Ffion Davies (12)
Ysgol Gyfun Y Cymer, Rhondda

168

Love

Love is more than just
A word,
Love is a meaning;
A life-changing meaning.

L-o-v-e, this is what
Love means to me:
A relationship that means
Everything (and more).

Love means a lot more
Than just a box of chocolates!
It means everything (and more).

Georgia Toms (12)
Ysgol Gyfun Y Cymer, Rhondda

Love

Your eyes are stars, so bright,
I dream of the day you'll hold me tight.

You're like an angel from above,
You're the only one I want to love.

I've been dreaming of your love for too long,
Just give me a chance, we'll work it out if things go wrong.

But it's time to face reality.
You don't want to know me!

Molly Evans (12)
Ysgol Gyfun Y Cymer, Rhondda

Young Writers Information

We hope you have enjoyed reading this book - and that you will continue to enjoy it in the coming years.

If you like reading and writing poetry drop us a line, or give us a call, and we'll send you a free information pack.

Alternatively if you would like to order further copies of this book or any of our other titles, then please give us a call or log onto our website at www.youngwriters.co.uk.

Young Writers Information
Remus House
Coltsfoot Drive
Peterborough
PE2 9JX
(01733) 890066